Second Empire Architecture in Ontario in Colour Photos, Saving Our History One Photo at a Time

Photography
by Barbara Raué
©2019

Series Name: Architectural Styles

Book 2: Second Empire Style

Cover photo: Kingston Book 5 – 116 Bagot Street, Page 28

©All the photos in this book have been taken with my cameras. I own the rights to them.

Second Empire, 1860-1880 – The mansard roof is the most noteworthy feature of this style and is evidence of the French origins. Projecting central towers and one or two-storey bays can also be present.

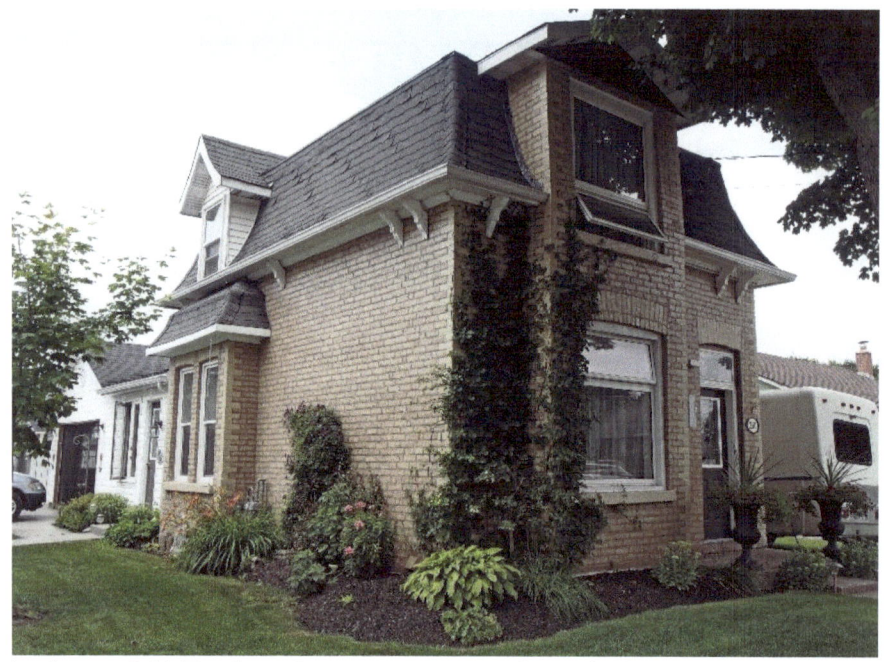

Arthur - 261 Tucker Street – mansard roof, dormers, cornice brackets

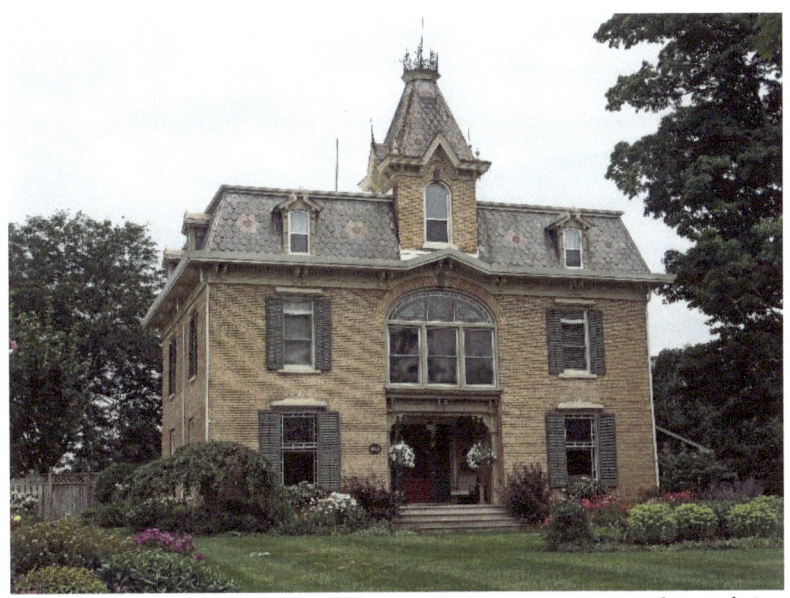

Aylmer Book 1 - 445 Talbot Street West – mansard roof, iron cresting, window hoods on dormers

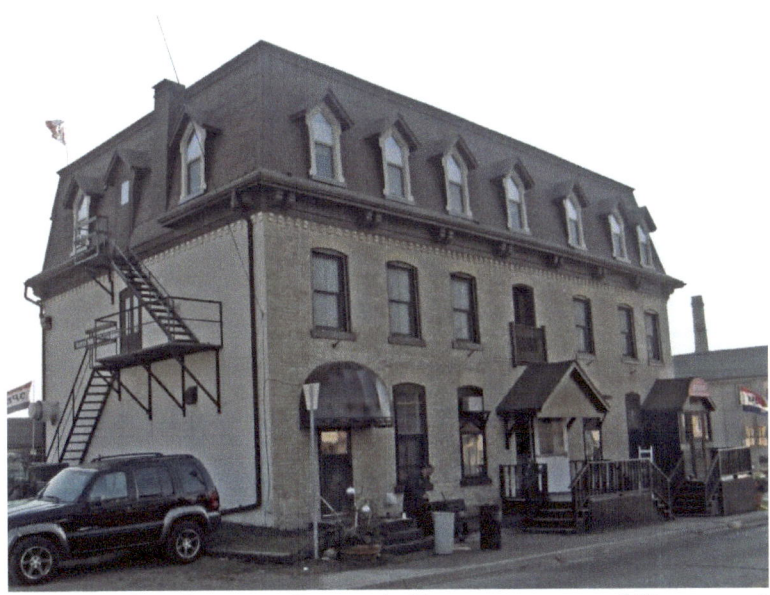

Ayr - 99 Stanley Street - Queen's Restaurant and Tavern since 1856, mansard roof, dormers, paired cornice brackets, dentil moulding

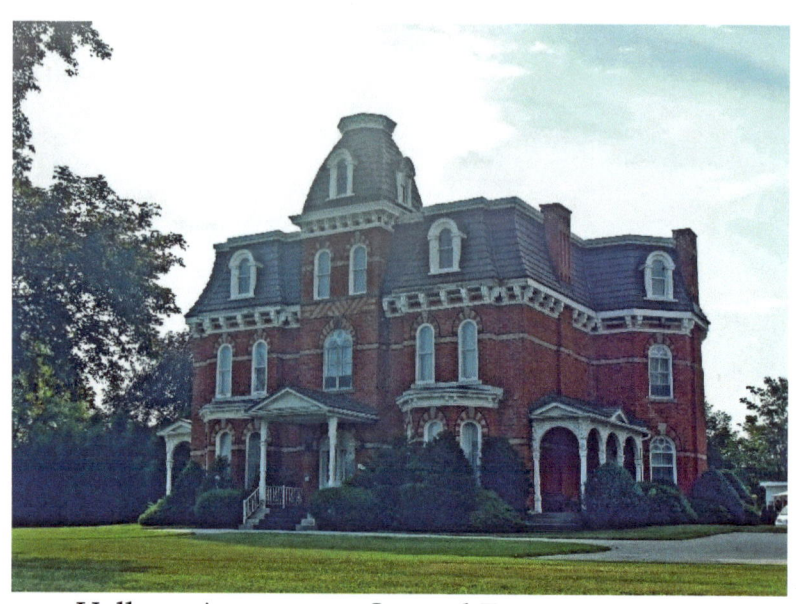

Beaver Valley - A gorgeous Second Empire style mansion in Markdale

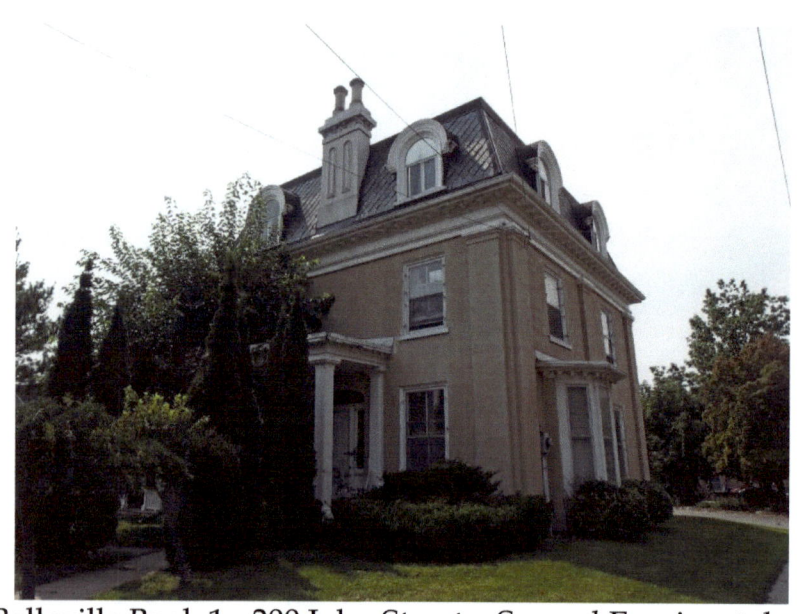

Belleville Book 1 - 200 John Street – Second Empire style – mansard roof, dormers with window hoods, tall chimneys, bay window

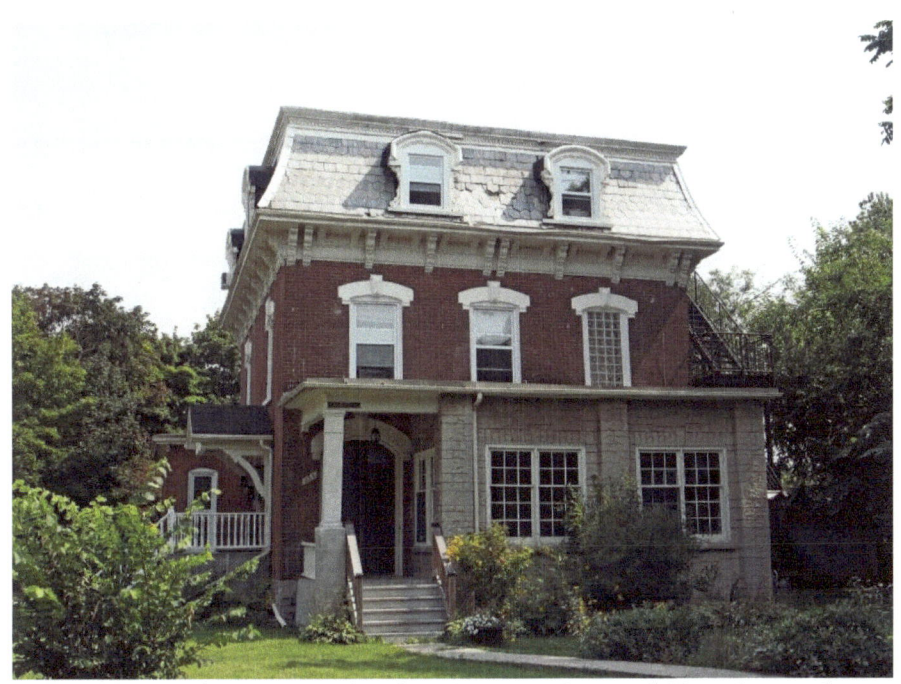

Belleville Book 2 - 233 Charles Street – Second Empire style – mansard roof with dormers and window hoods, brackets and decorative cornice, keystones

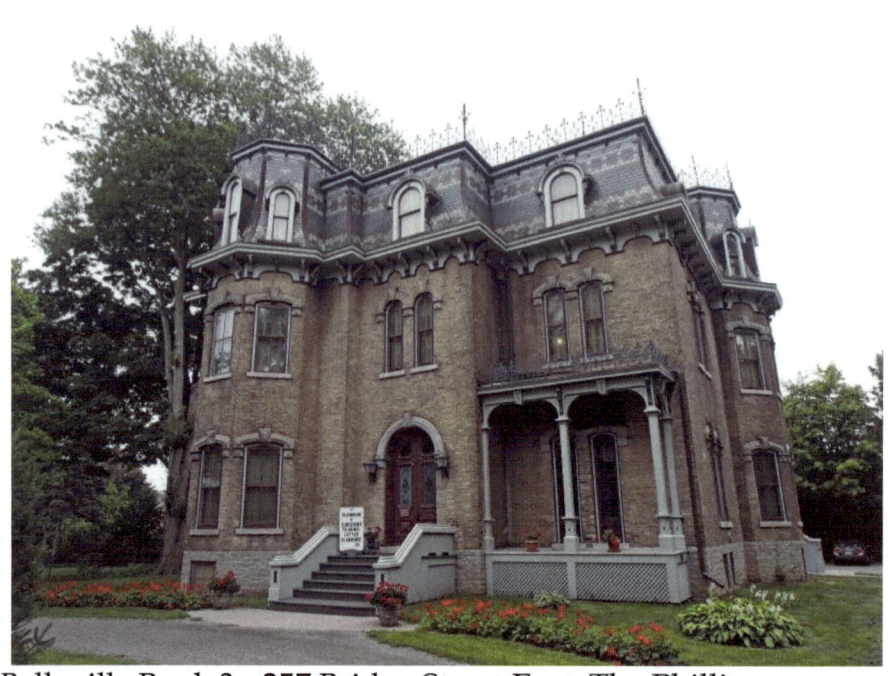

Belleville Book 3 - 257 Bridge Street East, The Phillips-Burrows-Faulknor House - Glanmore National Historic Site - Harriet Phillips inherited this property from George Bleecker, her grandfather. Glanmore reflects the tastes of the well-to-do in late nineteenth century Canada. The grand house, built by local architect Thomas Hanley, was built in 1882-1883 for wealthy banker John Philpot Curran Phillips and his wife Harriet Ann Dougall, the daughter of Belleville's Judge Benjamin Dougall. It is in the Second Empire style with mansard roof with elaborate cornices and brackets, dormer windows, iron cresting, a built-in gutter system, and multi-colored slate. The 9,000 square foot home cost $7,000 to build in 1883. The impressive suspended walnut staircase cost $62.50.

The Reception Room was used to receive callers. In the 19th century, strict etiquette was followed. Visitors upon their arrival presented their calling cards to a servant and then waited in the Reception Room. If the hostess was available, the visitor was shown in. If the hostess was unavailable, then a calling card was left in a card receiver.

The table in the Dining Room with ten leaves, chairs, side board, and fireplace mantle are original to the house. Mr. and Mrs. Phillips hosted elegant dinners in this setting. The Breakfast Room and Service Hall is an informal room where the family ate casual meals.

The Billiard and Card Rooms were added to the house sometime after 1900. The smaller Card Room was used for board and card games.

The North Drawing Room was used by Mr. and Mrs. Phillips for entertaining. Ornate columns divide the North and South areas of the double drawing room. The rooms could also be used as a ballroom when the carpets and furniture were removed. The coffered ceilings feature molded ornamental plaster and hand-painted designs.

The Master Bedroom and Bathroom is an expansive room used by Mr. and Mrs. Phillips. The original bathroom was one of the first in Belleville to be fitted with indoor plumbing, and has a copper-lined tub. A water storage tank above the room collected rain water that was used to supply fixtures with cold water. Additional water was heated downstairs and pumped up to the bathroom.

Glanmore had seven fireplaces that burned coal or gas which meant that fire tending and its associated tasks were an important and laborious part of the maid's daily routine. Rising at five or six in the morning, the maid's first job was to clean the grates and light the fires, as well as prepare a hot morning beverage for the household. At the end of the day, the maid banked the fires, piling the coals to ensure that the fireplaces would heat the house well into the night.

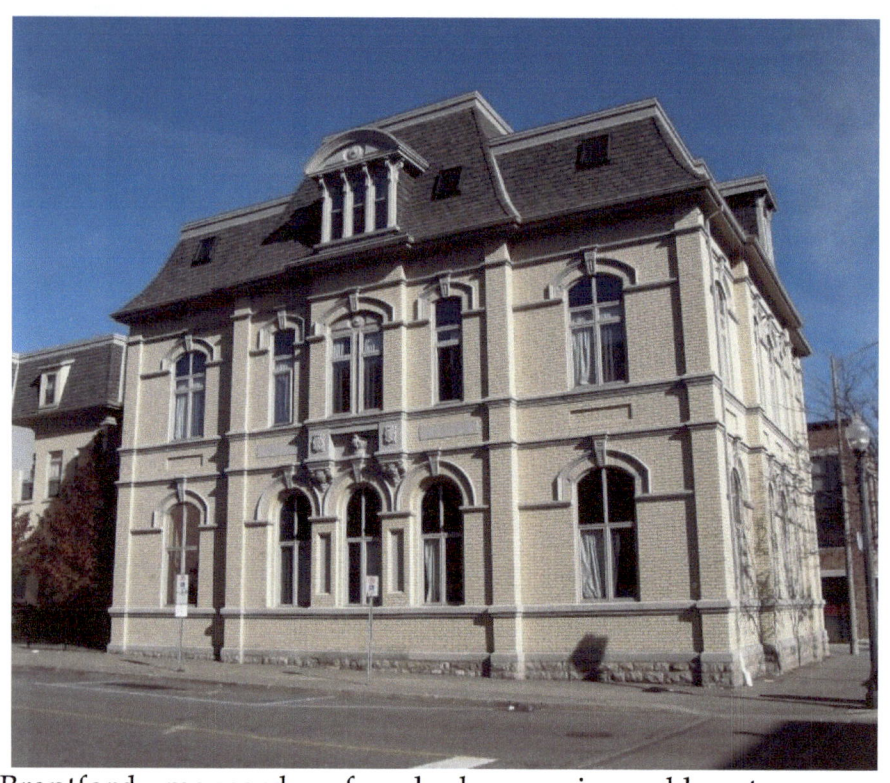

Brantford - mansard roof, arched voussoirs and keystones

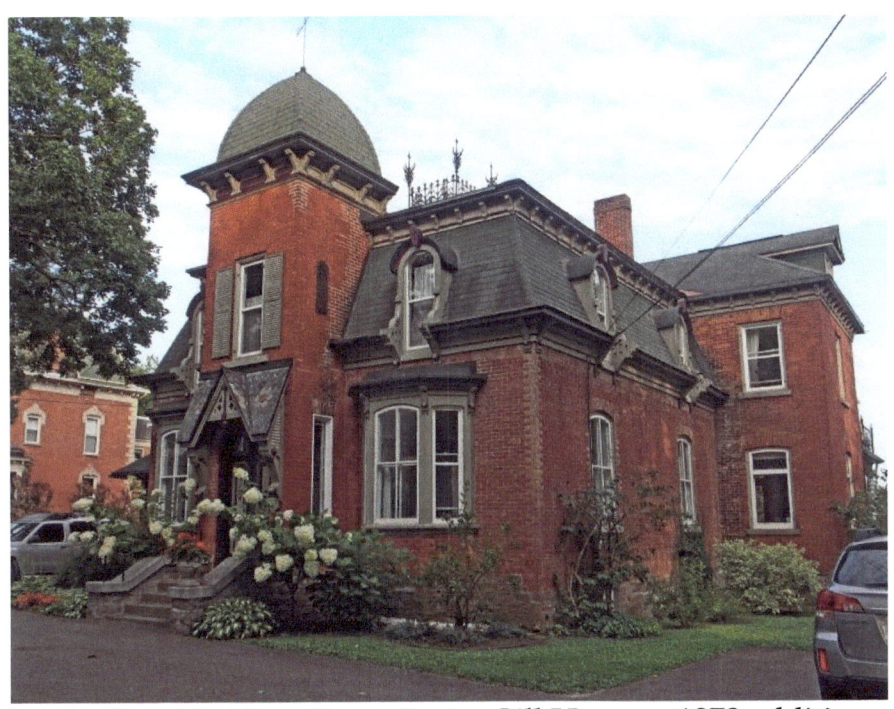

Brockville - 181 King Street East – Gill House – 1878 additions of roof and wings - mansard roof, dormers, window hoods with keystones, iron cresting around rooftop balcony, central tower, bay windows

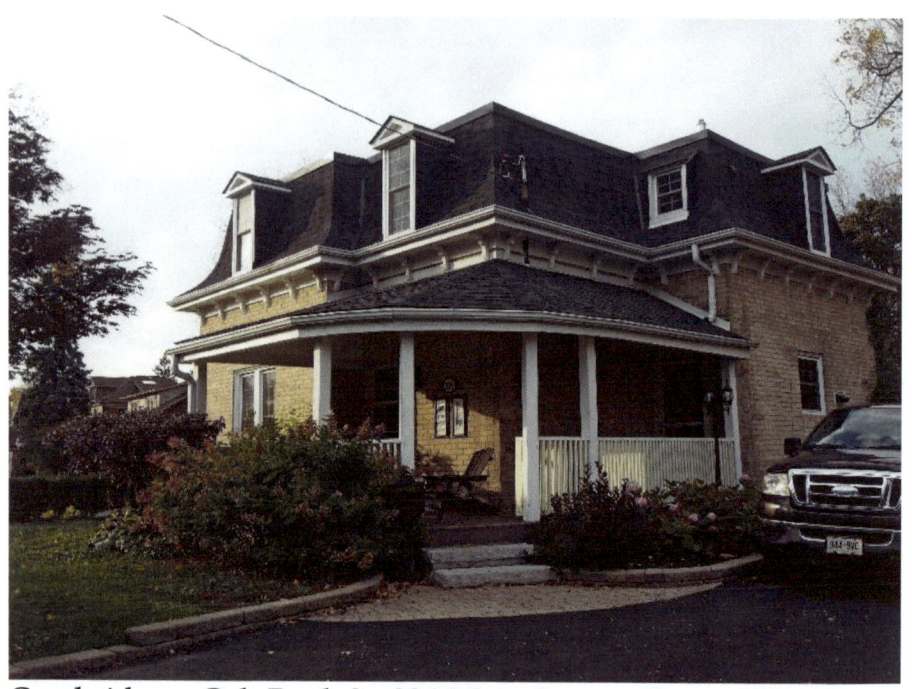

Cambridge – Galt Book 2 - 234 Main Street – Second Empire style – mansard roof with dormers, cornice brackets, yellow brick

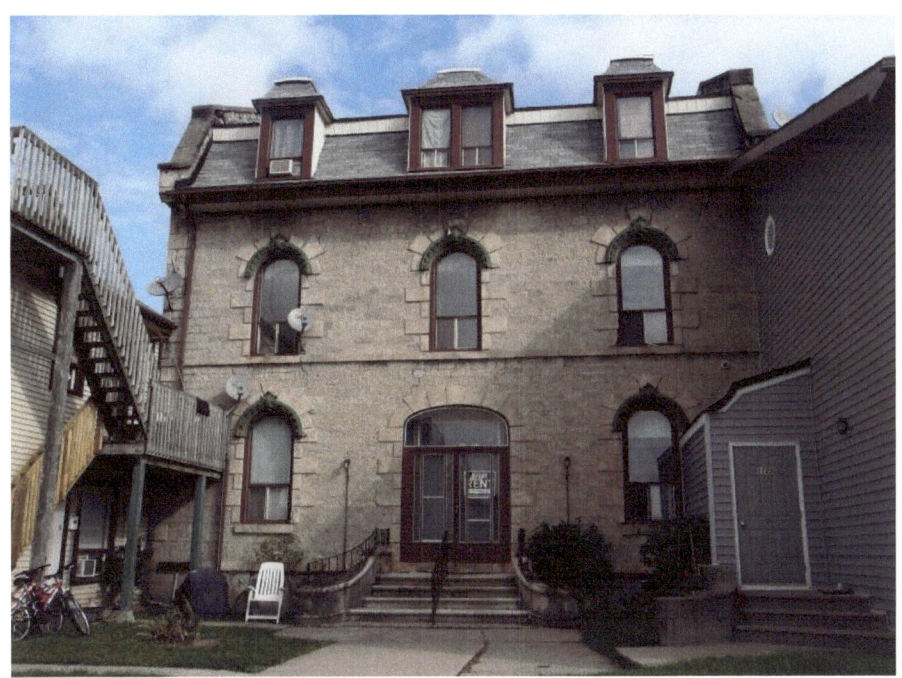

Cambridge – Preston - 1107 King Street – c. 1876 – Second Empire style with mansard roof with dormers, decorative brickwork around windows, arched window hoods with acroterion keystones

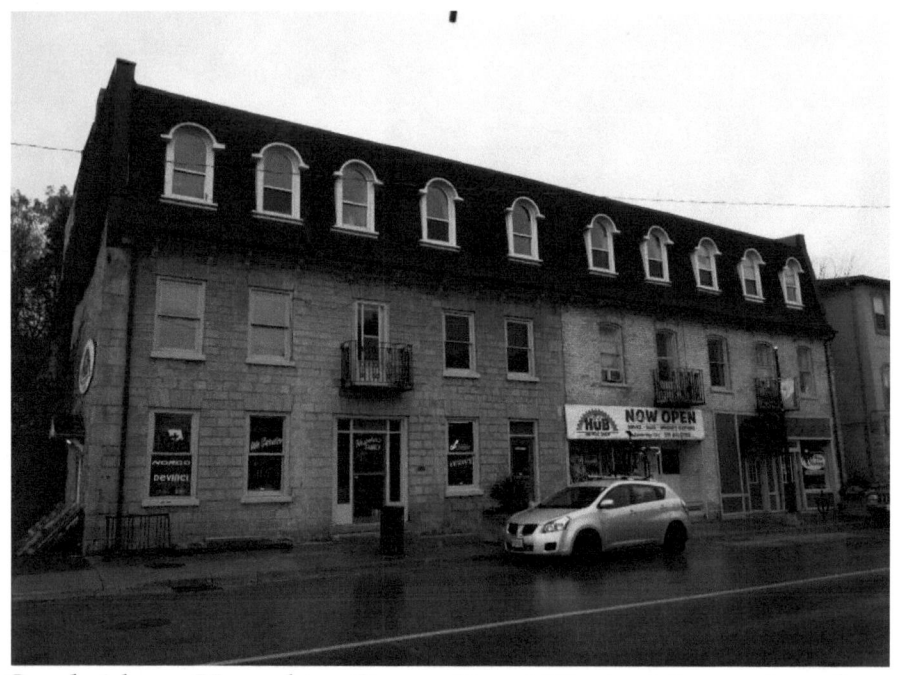

Cambridge – Hespeler - Queen Street West – Mansard roof with dormers

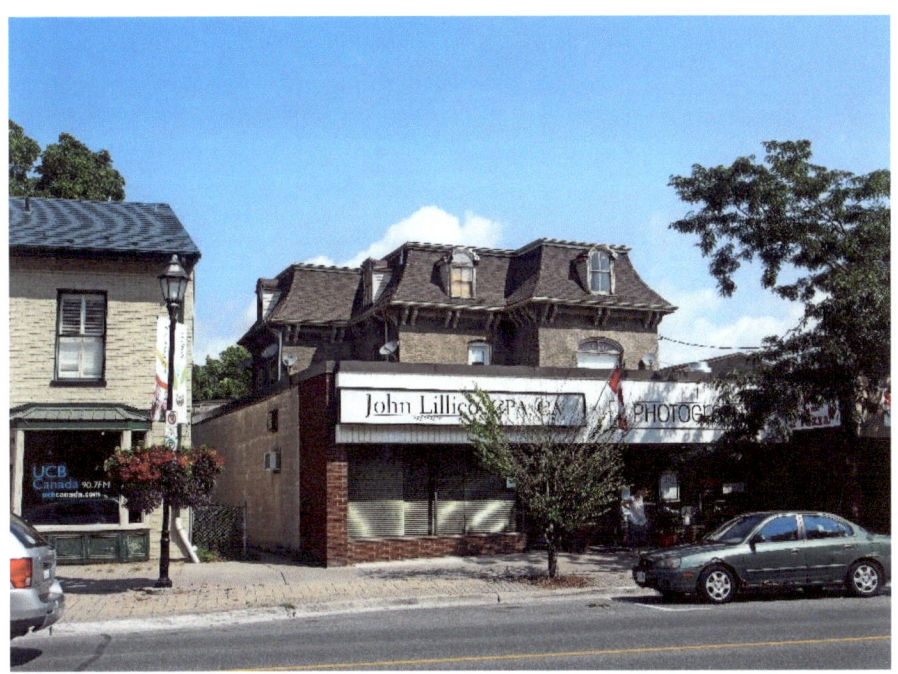

Cobourg Book 1 – 144 King Street West - The Second Empire-style home behind the Shawarma House was built in 1874 by William Battell, a local builder who later became a mayor of Cobourg. It once had stables, a coach house and an elaborate fence in front. William Beattie, the minister of St. Andrew's Presbyterian Church, was a lodger here and purchased the house after Battell's death. When war broke out in 1914, Beattie enlisted as a chaplain of the 40th Regiment of the Cobourg Battalion and rose to become the chaplain of the entire 2nd Division. His letters from the front sent to the local newspapers comprise a remarkable chronicle of the war. In describing his first impression of the Western Front, he wrote: "Imagine trying to live for over a year in the trenches which you have seen workmen in Cobourg digging when laying sewers." After the war, Beattie moved to Ottawa and in 1956 the house was converted to a Canadian Tire store and the front addition has been a retail space ever since.

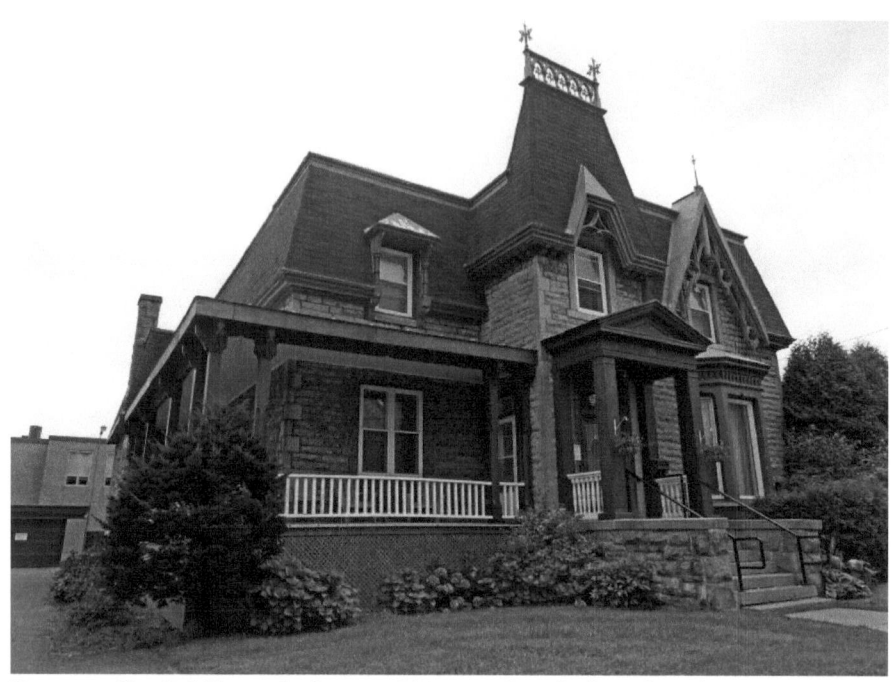

Cornwall - 36 Fourth Street West – St. Columban's Rectory - Second Empire domestic architecture with mansard roof and detailing; window hood, trim on gable, bay window, cornice brackets; open railing on porch and wraparound verandah

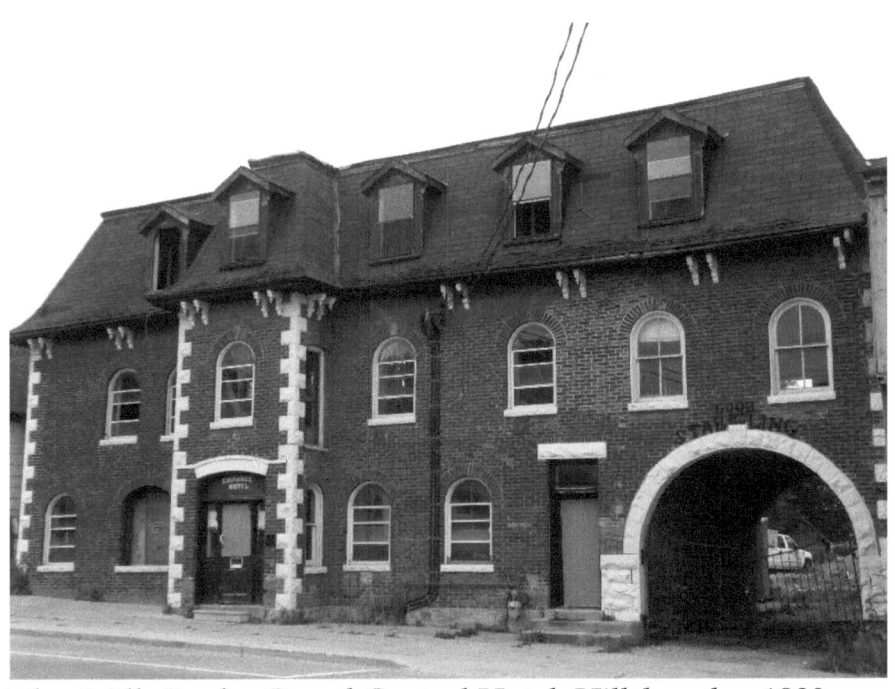

Eden Mills Book - Grand Central Hotel, Hillsburgh – 1880s – originally it was a carriage works, transformed into a hotel, served as a bank since the early 1900s - Second Empire – mansard roof with dormers, corner quoins, paired cornice brackets

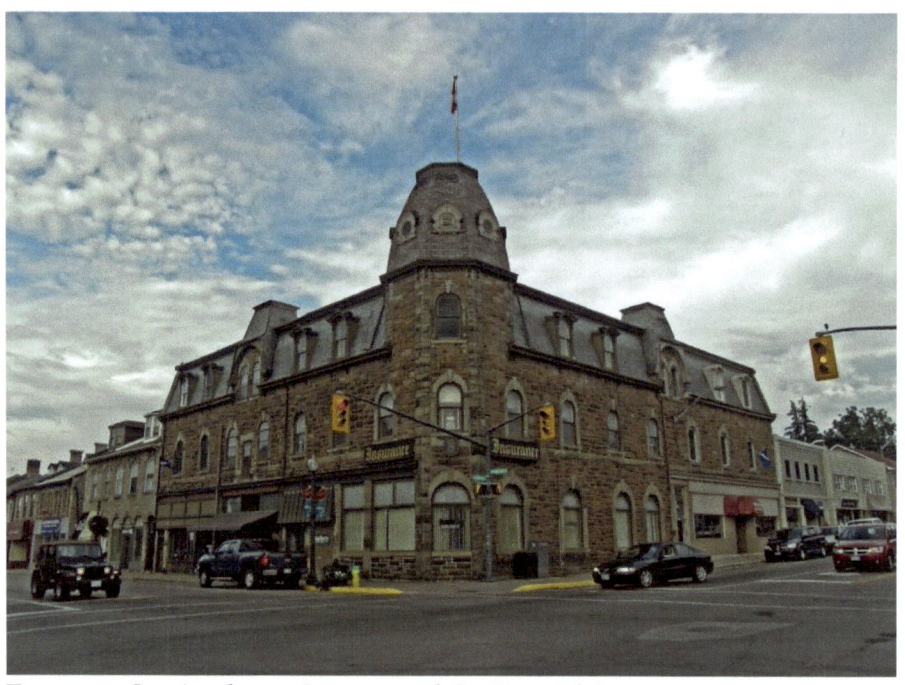

Fergus - St. Andrew Street and St. David Street corner – Second Empire style – mansard roof with dormers, window hoods four-storey tower

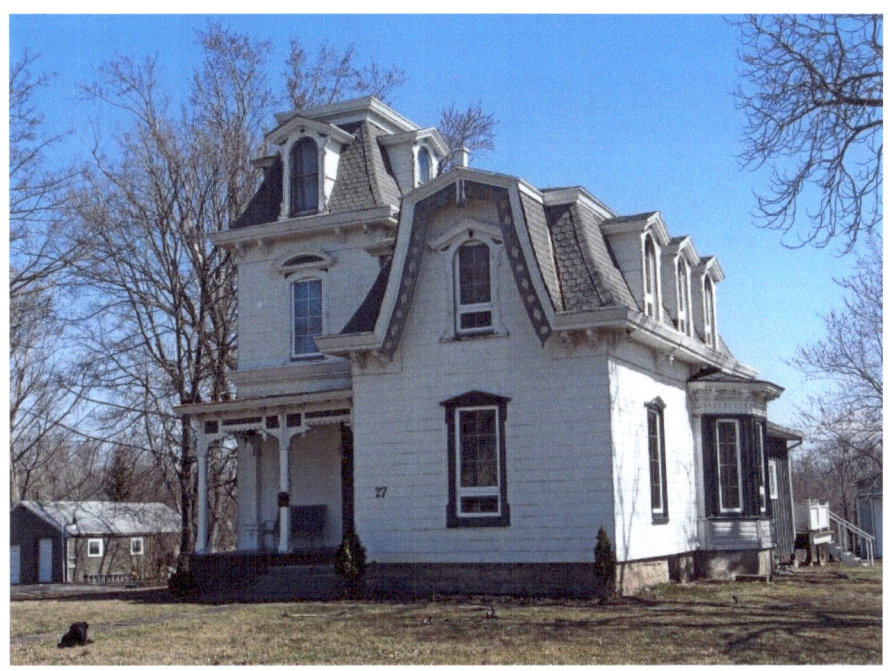

Fisherville, Nanticoke, Selkirk Book - 27 Erie Street South, Selkirk – James Cooper built this house in 1870. In 1878 he sold it to George Hoover. The frame house has irregular massing and is in the Second Empire style. It has an oversized horseshoe dormer with bargeboard and finial, elaborate window molds with pediments. The three-storey tower has four dormers in the mansard roof. The Fess family purchased it in 1947.

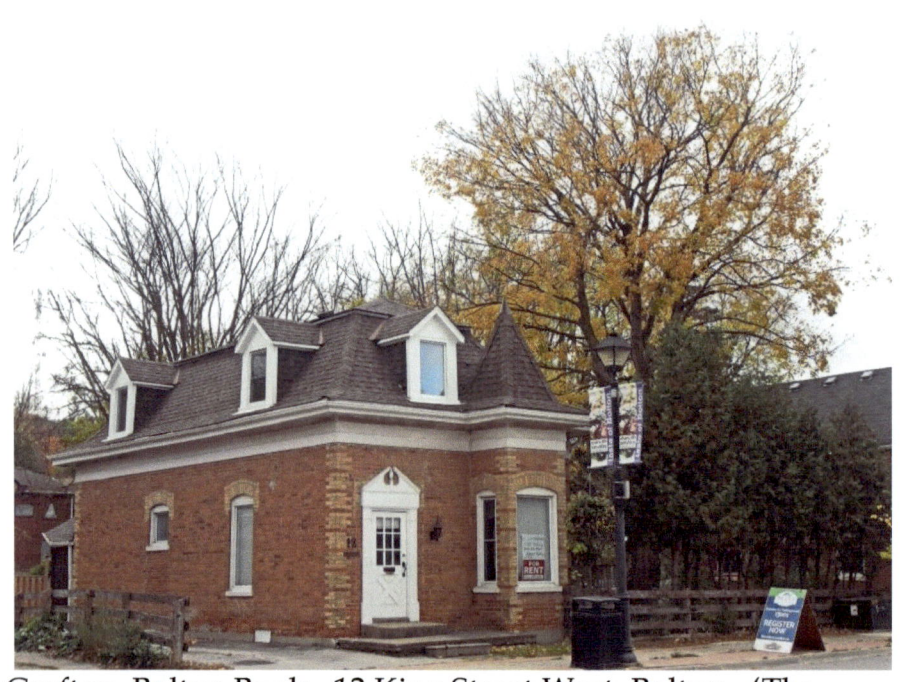

Grafton, Bolton Book - 12 King Street West, Bolton - 'The Castle' - mid-1870s - A rare example of the Second Empire style with its mansard roof and square projecting bay, this house was built for Ann Roberts. Ownership passed to her son William L. Roberts in 1893 and from him to Margaret Jane Osburn in 1907. Olga and Wesley Strong and their son Charlie lived here until 1923 when Wes's health failed. Charlie lived to 100 and was a great Bolton story teller. Mrs. Dickson owned the house in the 1930s and left it to her daughter Pearl who raised eight children here with her husband Lee Morrison.

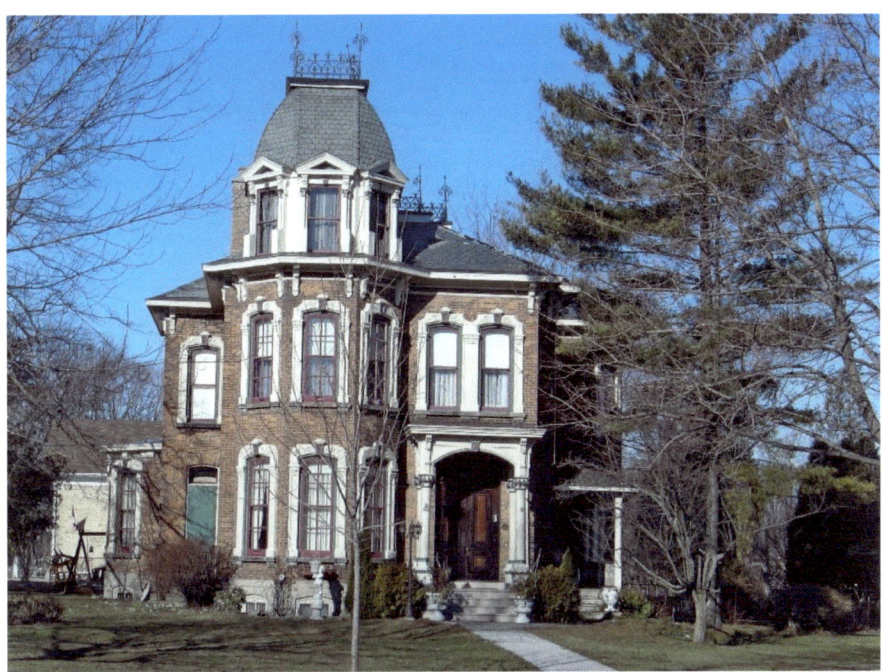

Goderich - 20 Wellington Street South - The "Strachan House" was built by Adam McVicar, builder of the lighthouse, in 1880. A schooner brought 40,000 bricks to Goderich to construct this mansion for Donald Strachan, a prominent businessman. The Second Empire house features a mansard roof of patterned slate, and a tower crowned with iron cresting, and intricately molded window headings.

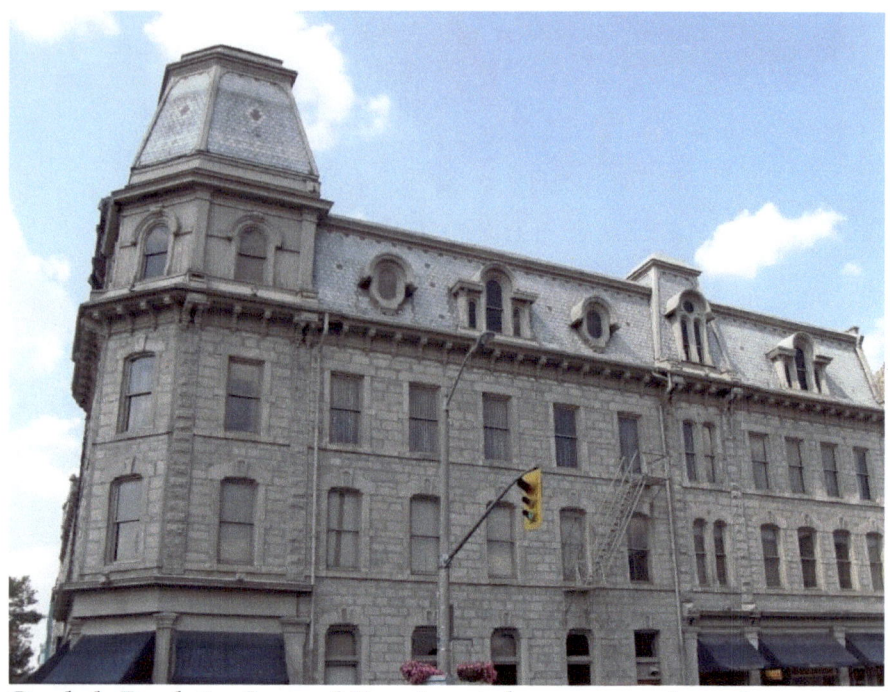

Guelph Book 1 - Second Empire style - mansard roof, trichromatic tile work, window hoods on dormers, cornice brackets

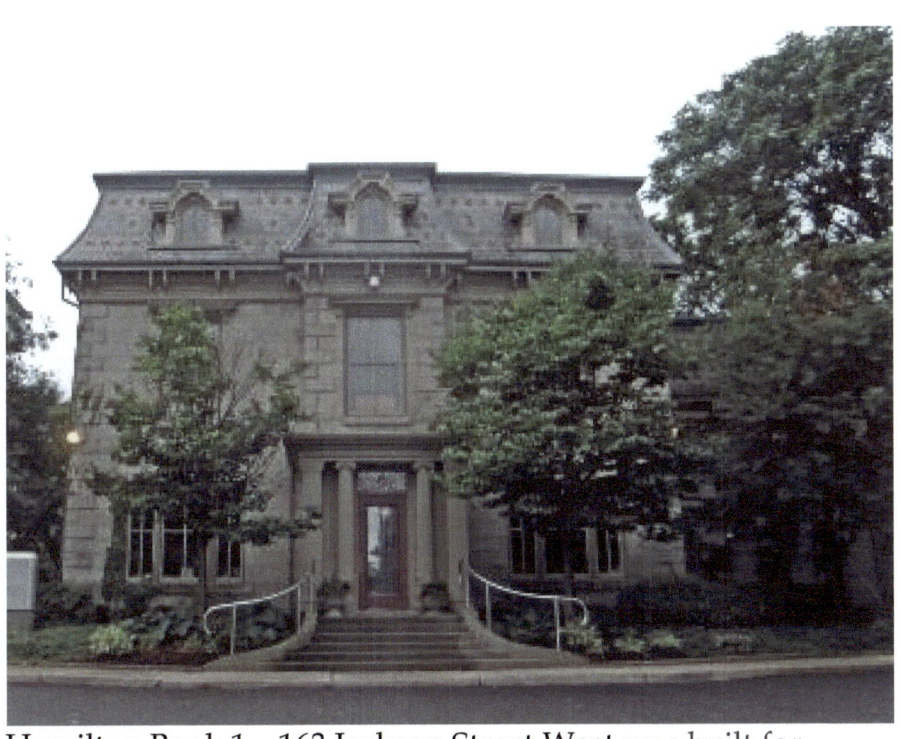

Hamilton Book 1 – 163 Jackson Street West was built for pharmacist/entrepreneur Tristram Bickle c. 1850 – Second Empire style, mansard roof, dichromatic tile work; ionic capitals on pillars, cornice brackets, corner quoins. Bishop T.B. Fuller moved here in 1884. From 1892 to 1932, Southam newspapers owner William Southam lived here. In 1954, Ken Soble launched CHCH TV here.

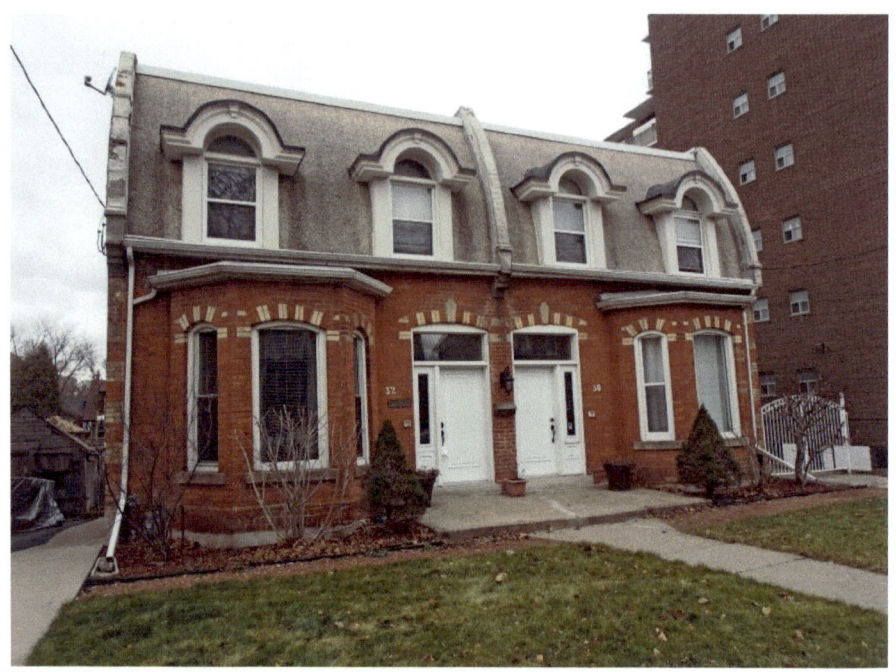

Hamilton Book 2 – 30-32 Erie Avenue – Second Empire, mansard roof, dormers with window hoods, dichromatic brickwork; Unit 32 Harry A. Ellis, Draftsman

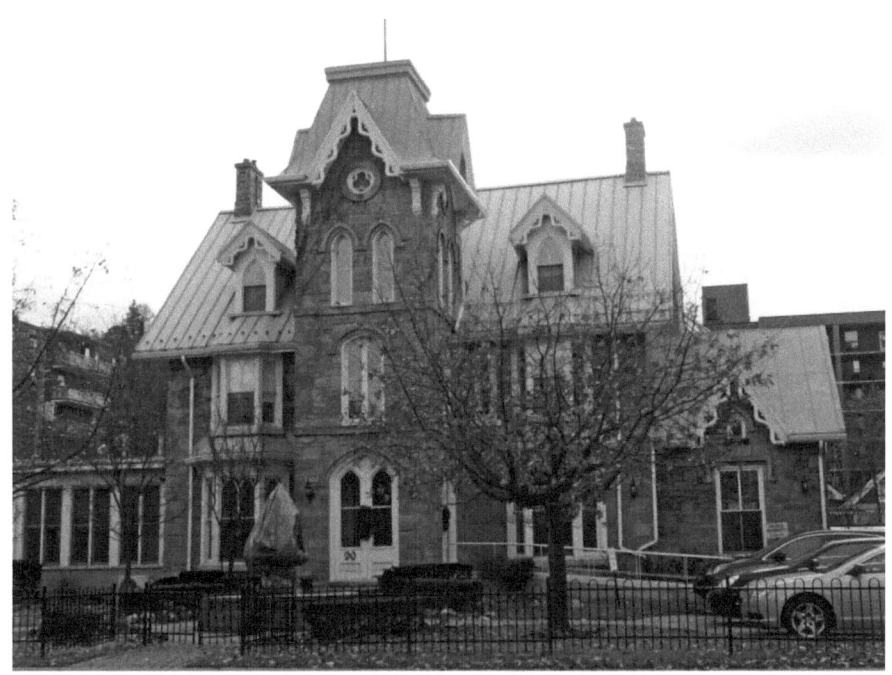

Hamilton Book 3 – Mansard-roofed three-storey tower - Frederick William Fearman was the son of a shoemaker who emigrated from England in 1833 with his parents at the age of eight. He started his business with a store selling smoked and salted meats on Hughson Street between King and King William, moved to a MacNab Street North location near the farmers' market, and eventually expanded to become W. Fearman Packing Company Limited, with a large factory at Rebecca Street and Ferguson Avenue on the Grand Trunk Railway line. The company slaughtered, hung, salted, smoked and canned pork, beef, veal and lamb for shipment around the world. Fearman built his mansion, "Ivey Lodge", at 90 Stinson Street in 1863. It is three-storey, limestone block with a Mansard-roofed tower as its front entrance; it has bay and arched windows, dormers, verge board trim, and a green metal roof.

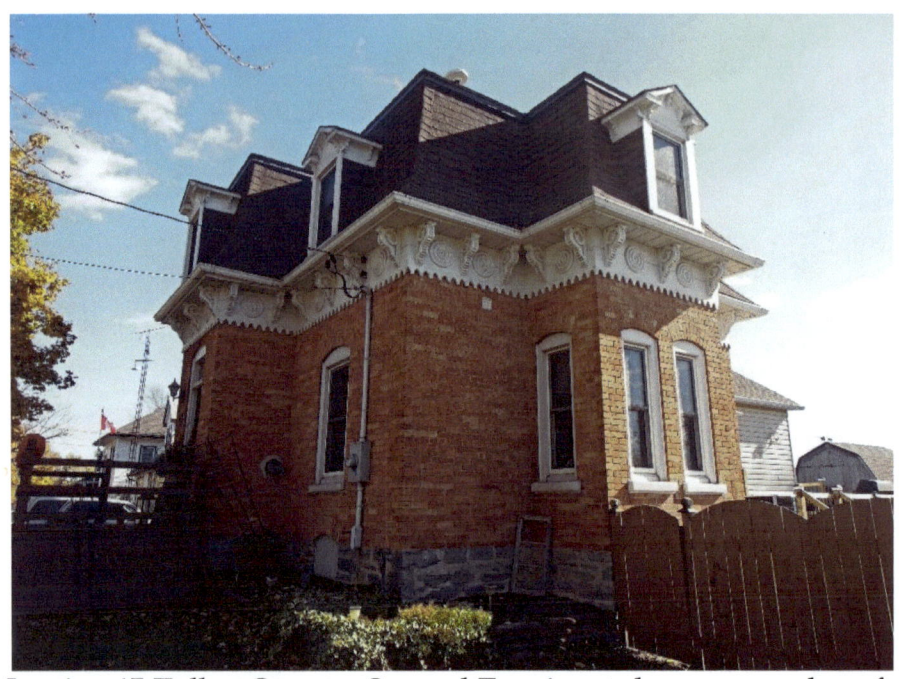

Jarvis - 45 Talbot Street – Second Empire style – mansard roof, dormers in roof, single cornice brackets, cornice return on small gables on window dormers

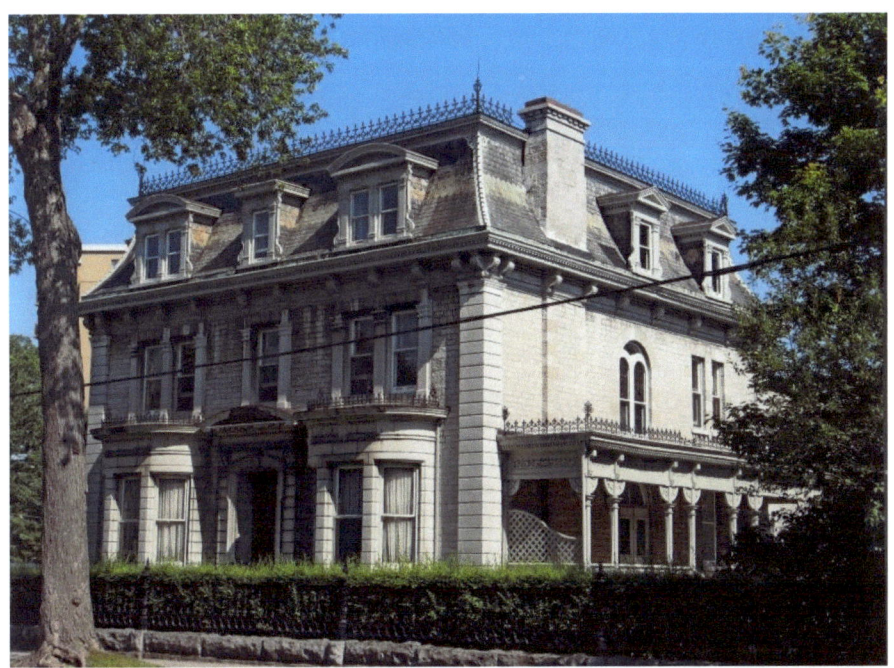

Kingston Book 1 – 85 King Street East – 1877 – three storey Victorian Second Empire style stone mansion – mansard roof, dormers, verandah, bay windows

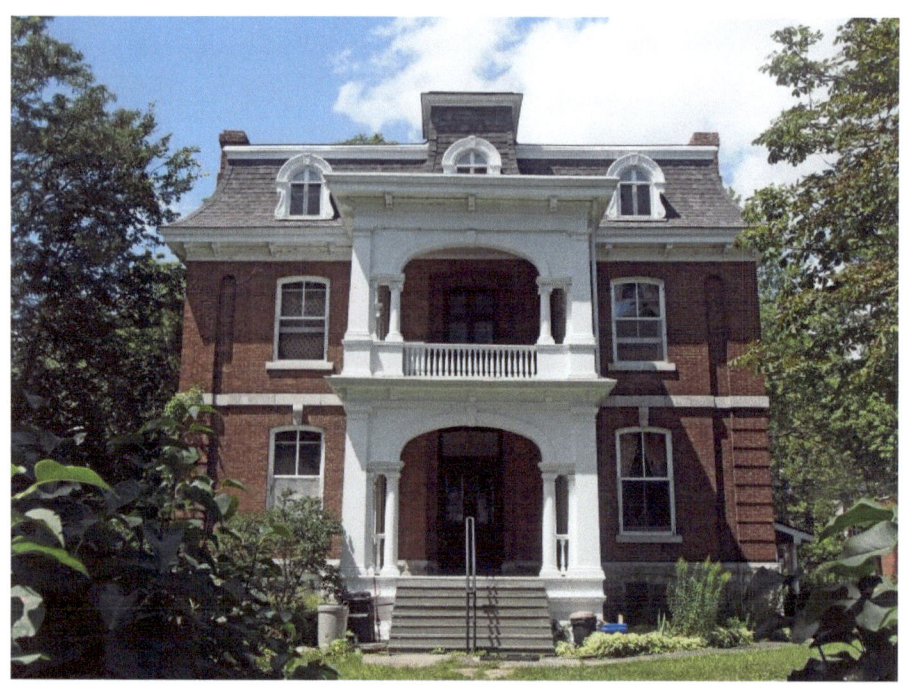

Kingston Book 2 – 12 Wellington Street – Second Empire, mansard roof, dormers with window hoods, two-storey central verandahs – Doric columns on first storey with semi-circular arch with keystone; Ionic columns on second storey with identical arch

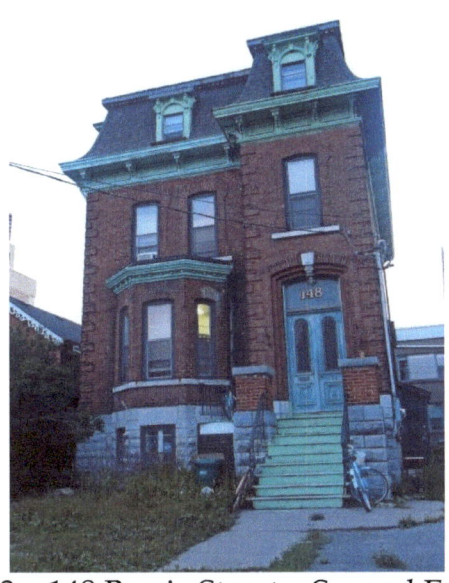

Kingston Book 3 – 148 Barrie Street – Second Empire – mansard roof, dormers with window hoods, corner quoins, bay window

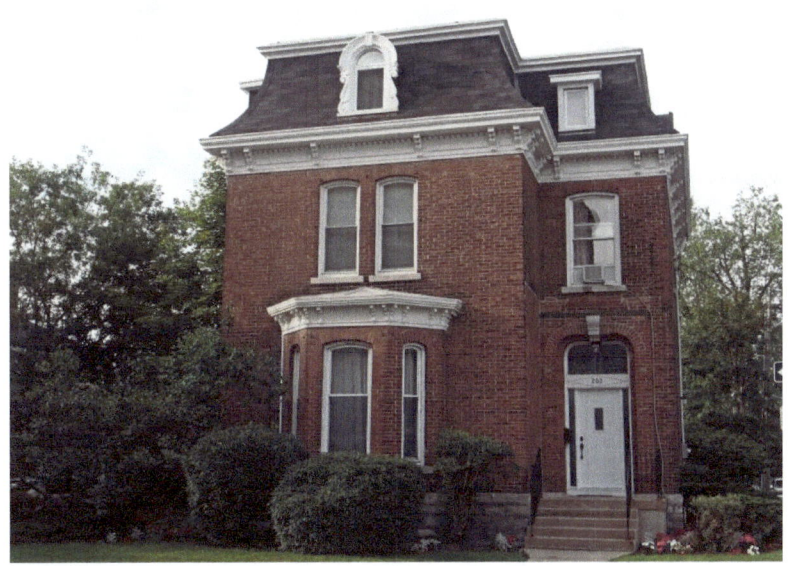

Kingston Book 4 – 202 Johnson Street – Second Empire style, Mansard roof, dormers, bay window, keystone above door

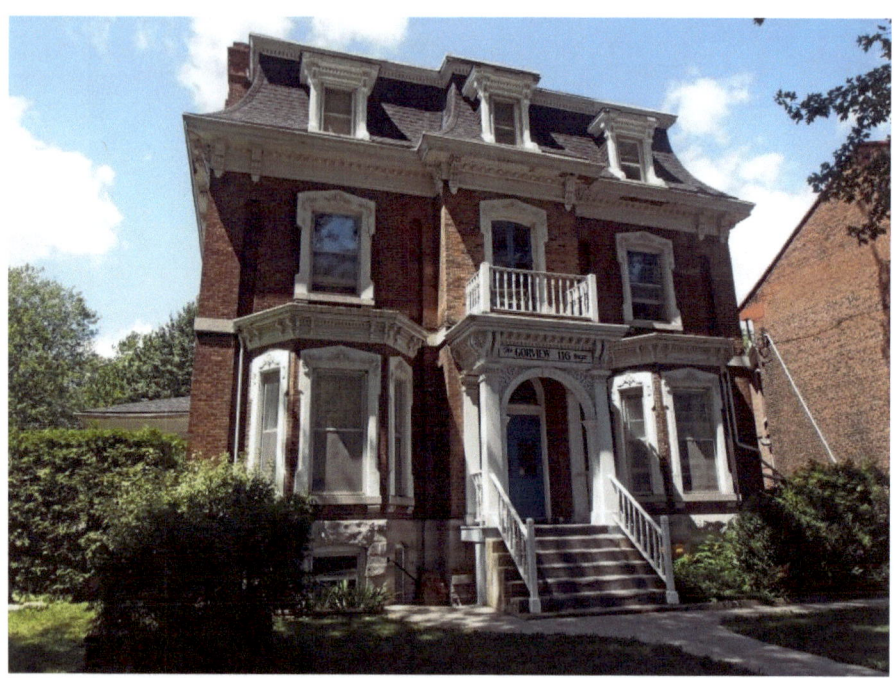

Kingston Book 5 – 116 Bagot Street – Second Empire, Mansard roof with dormers and window hoods, second floor balcony, bay windows, cornice brackets, dentil moulding, pillared entrance

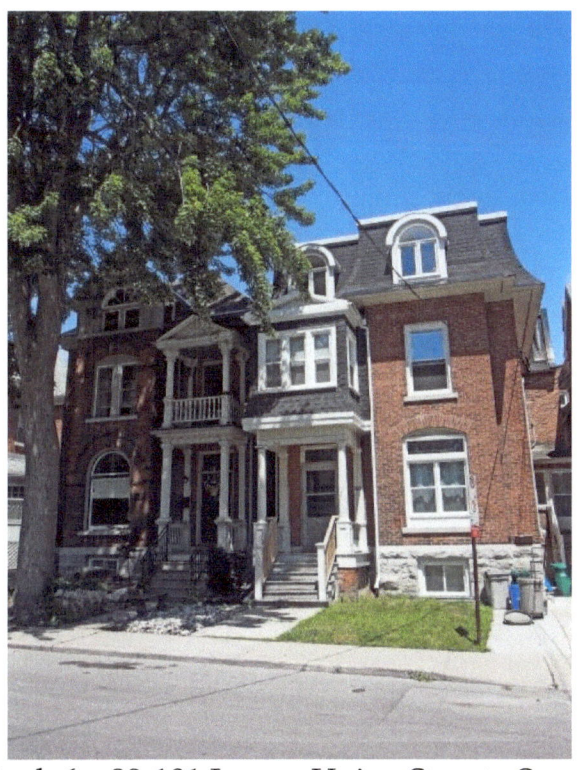

Kingston Book 6 – 99-101 Lower Union Street - Second Empire, Mansard roof, dormers, two-storied pillared porches with pediment, transom windows above doors

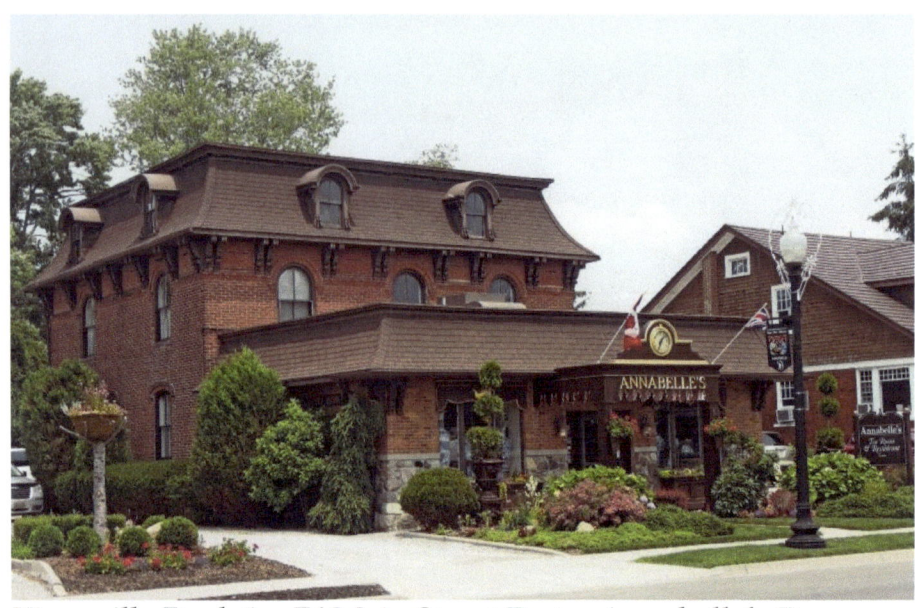

Kingsville Book 1 – 76 Main Street East – Annabelle's Tea House and Restaurant - Built in 1859 – Second Empire style – dormers with window hoods in mansard roof, paired cornice brackets. Anna Belle Miriah Brien Evans was Susanne's grandmother, for whom tea was an essential part of her day. Tea time for her grandma was an institution. At 4 o'clock, as matter-of-factly as anything done on a regular basis, she would proceed to the kitchen as if reminded by an internal clock. Susanne would get the small china tea set and set the table by the window in the dining room. There, as the sunlight streamed in, they would sip tea, have a biscuit, or two, and talk about the day. These are childhood memories that Susanne cherishes. In her honour, she created a place for people to spend time together and perhaps create lovely memories of their own. Tea time has a way of making an ordinary day an occasion.

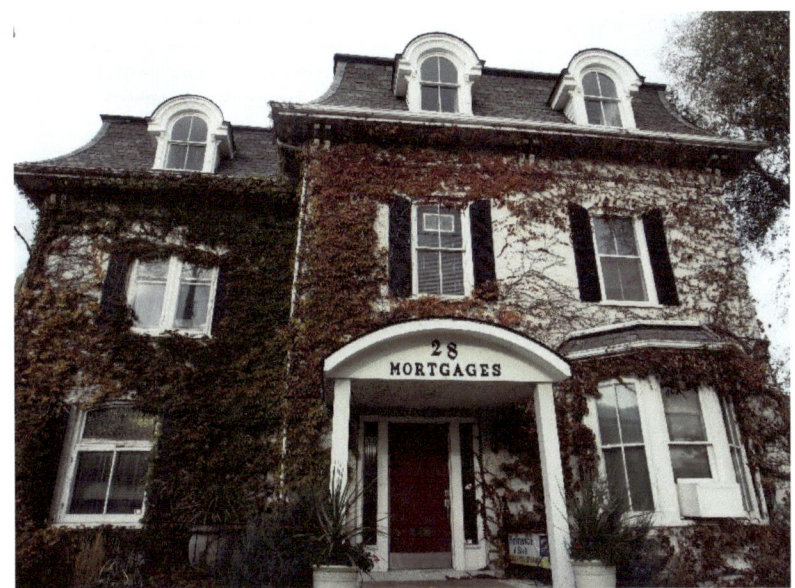

Kitchener Book 2 – 28 Weber Street West – Second Empire style – mansard roof, dormers in roof

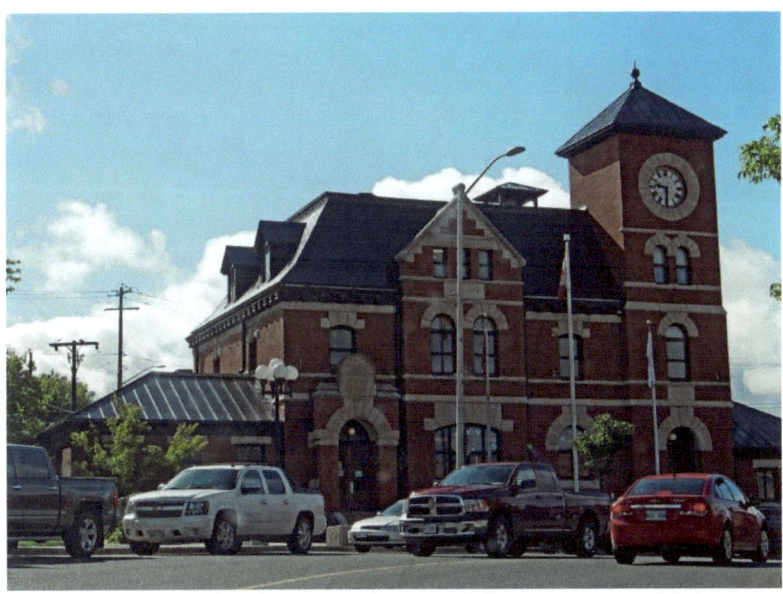

Lake Superior Book – Kenora Post Office – A.D. 1898 – Second Empire style – mansard roof with dormers, dichromatic brickwork, banding, three-storey clock tower

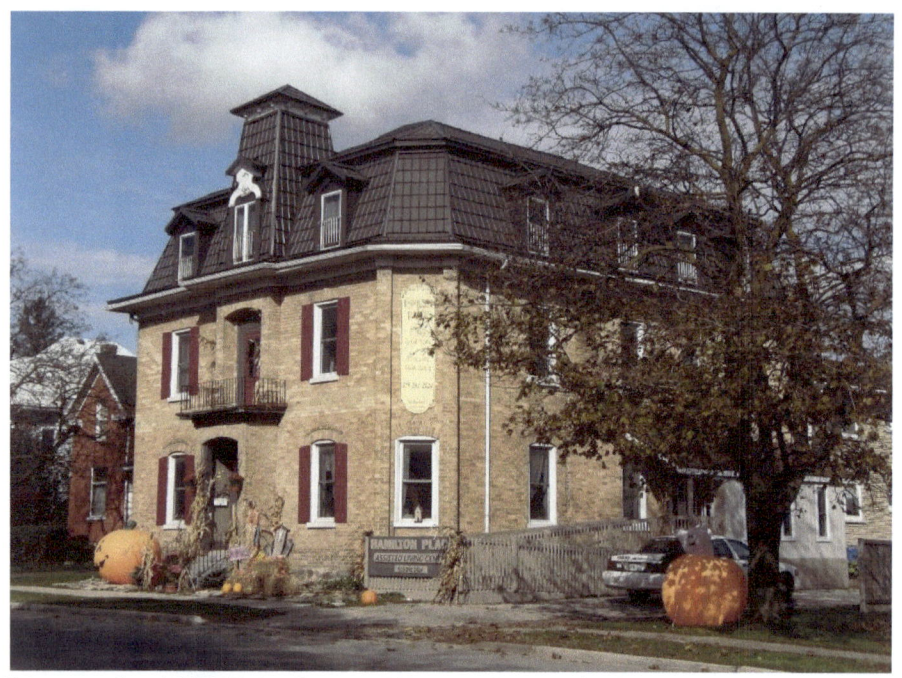

Listowel - 469 Main Street West – Second Empire style, Mansard roof, dormers with window hoods, built of Wallace brick – was once on edge of town and operated as the Last Chance Hotel – last chance for a drink before leaving town

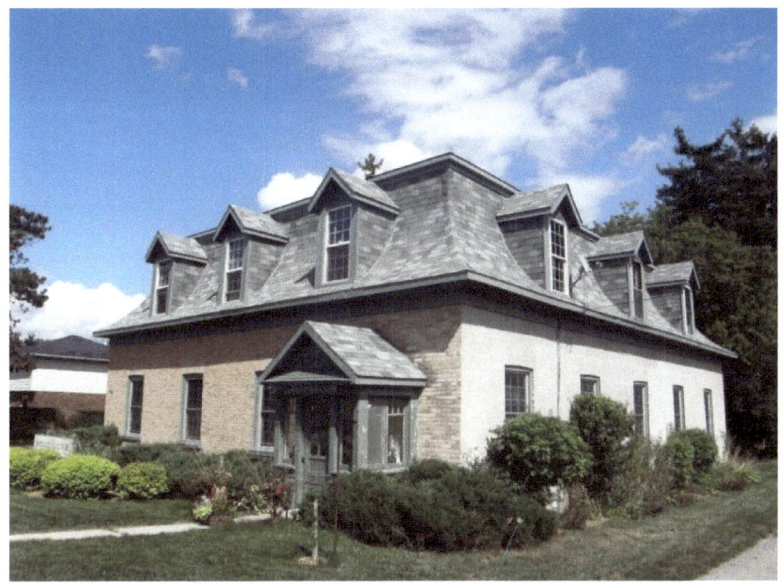

Lucknow - Campbell Street - Second Empire style, mansard roof with dormers

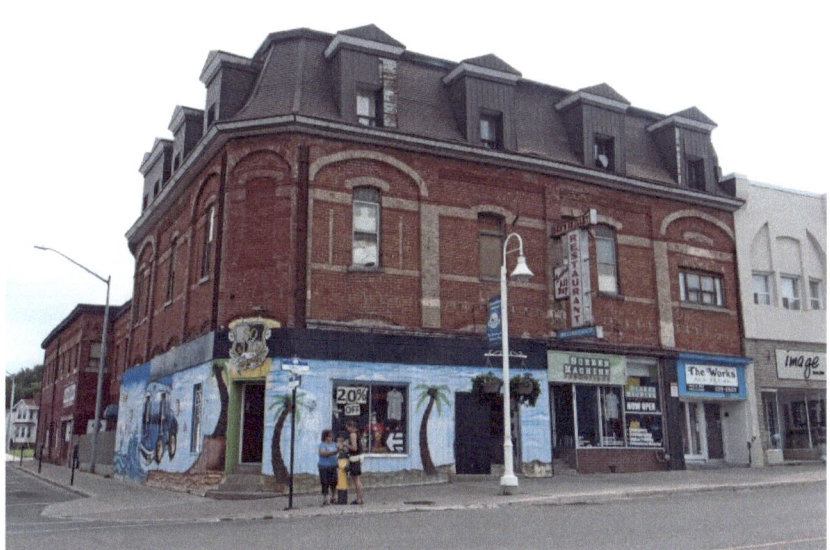

Midland Book 1 - 213-219 King Street – Second Empire – mansard roof, dormers, dichromatic brickwork

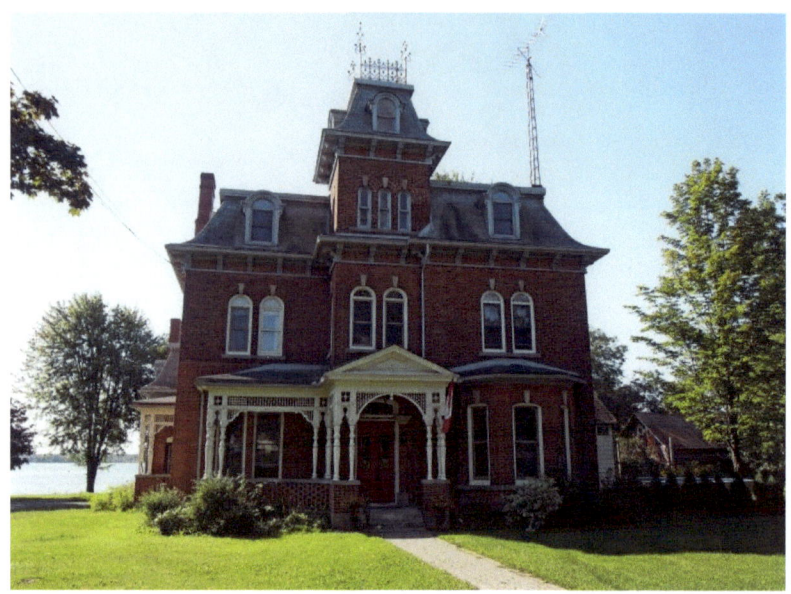

Morrisburg - 31 Lakeshore Drive – Second Empire style – projecting central tower, concave mansard roof, dormers; has eighteen stained glass windows, each with a different color scheme

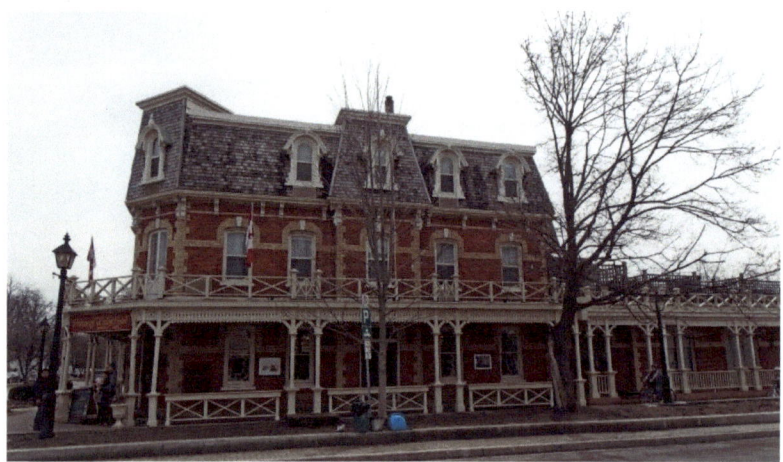

Niagara-on-the-Lake Book 1 - 6 Picton Street – The Prince of Wales Hotel established 1864 - Second Empire style, mansard roof, dormers, window hoods, dichromatic brickwork, cornice brackets, second floor balcony

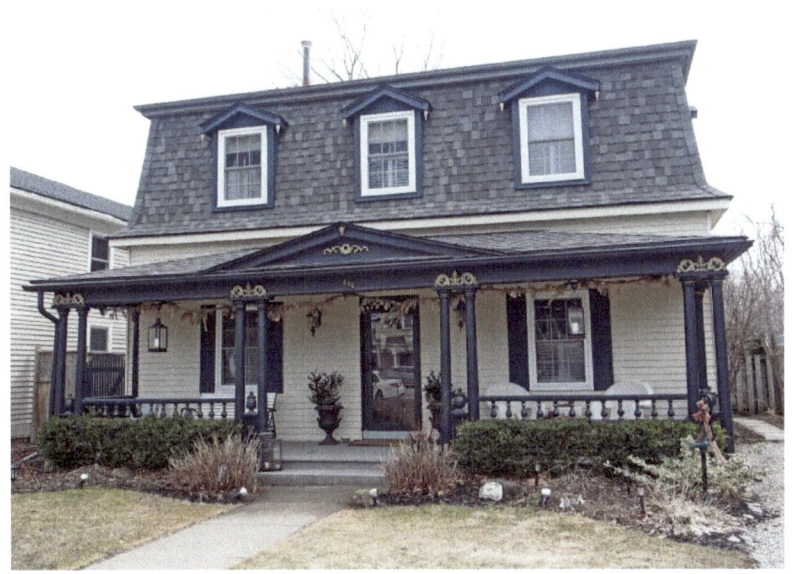

Niagara-on-the-Lake Book 2 - 236 King Street – Second Empire style, mansard roof, dormers

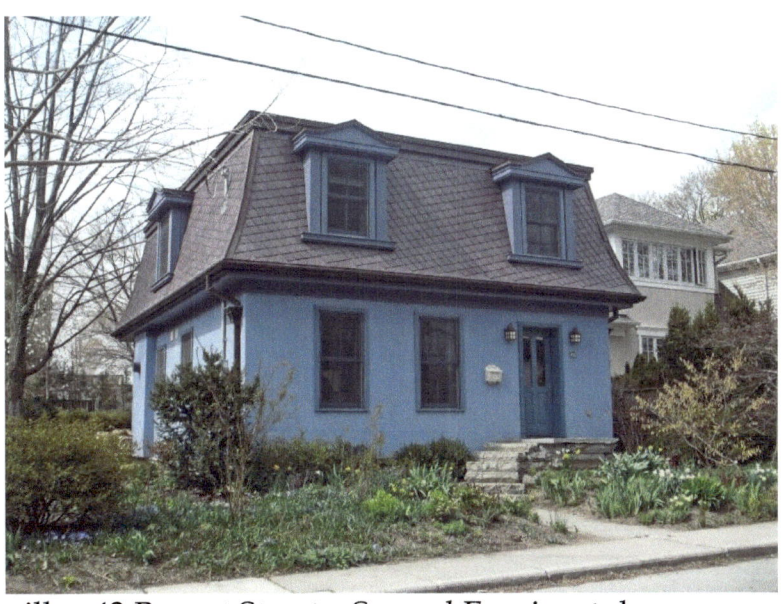

Oakville - 43 Burnet Street – Second Empire style - mansard roof, dormers

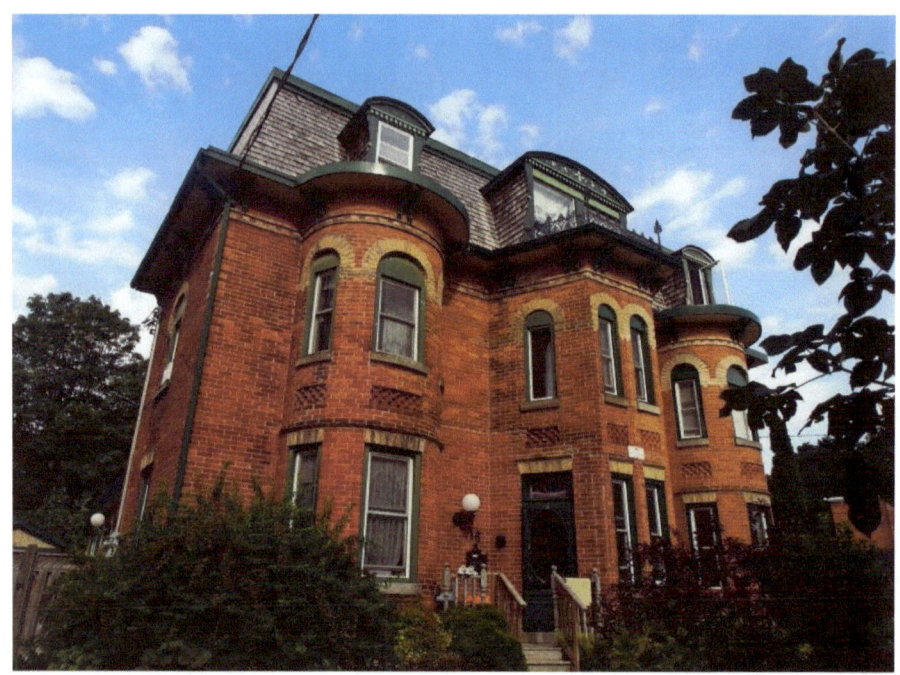

Orangeville Book 1 - 16-18 Wellington Street – King House c. 1888 - Second Empire style – large brick house, mansard roof, ornamental ironwork

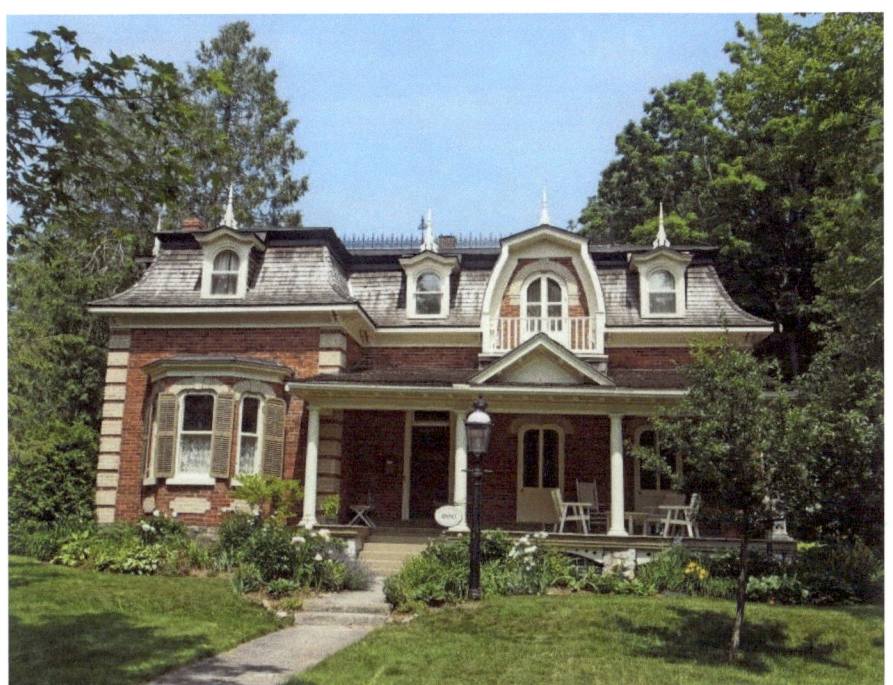

Orillia - #84 – E.J. McCrohan, Harness Maker c. 1880 - Second Empire style, mansard roof, iron cresting around roof, finials on dormers, second floor balcony, corner quoins

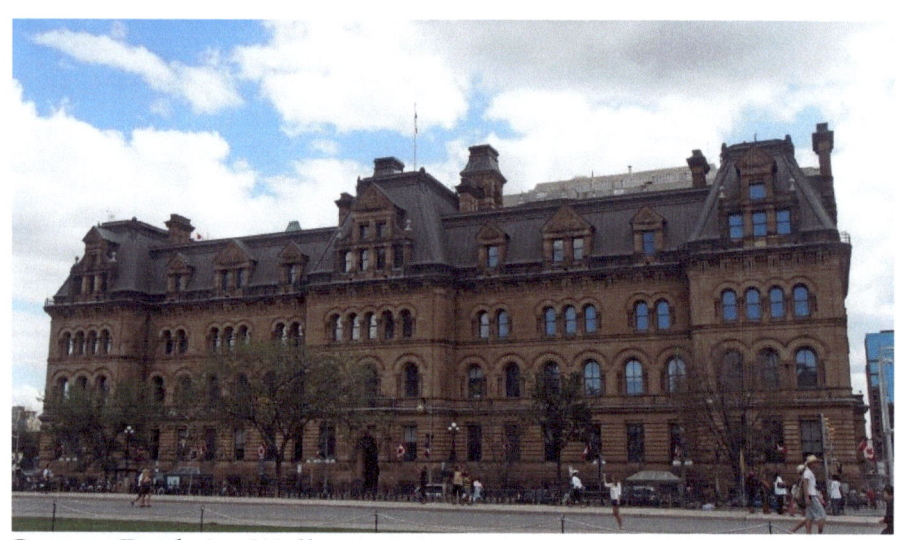

Ottawa Book 1 – Wellington Street - Langevin Block - is an office building facing Parliament Hill. As the home of the Privy Council Office and Office of the Prime Minister, it is the working headquarters of the executive branch of the Canadian government. The building is named after a Father of Confederation and cabinet minister Hector Langevin. Built of sandstone from a New Brunswick quarry between 1884 and 1889 - Second Empire style - Mansard roof, dormers, grotesque sculptures (fantastic or mythical figures used for decorative purposes)

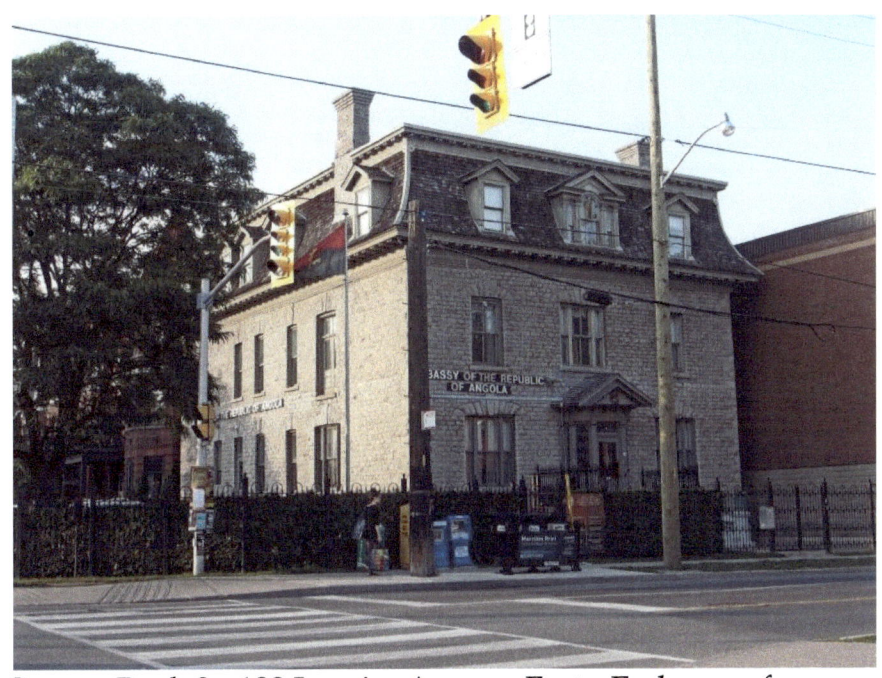

Ottawa Book 3 - 189 Laurier Avenue East - Embassy of Republic of Angola – Panet House – built in 1876 - Second Empire style – mansard roof, dormers

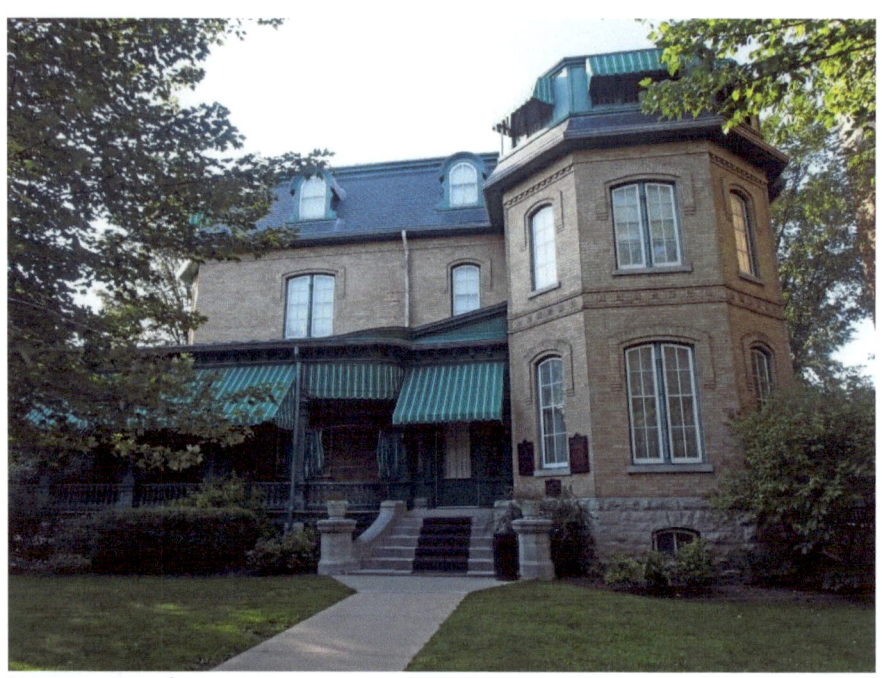

Ottawa Book 4 - 335 Laurier Avenue East - Laurier House – home of Prime Ministers Sir Wilfrid Laurier and William Lyon Mackenzie King – Victorian mansion built in 1878 – Second Empire/Italianate - Many distinguished guests were received at this house, such as King George VI, Sir Winston Churchill, Charles de Gaulle, and Franklin D. Roosevelt.

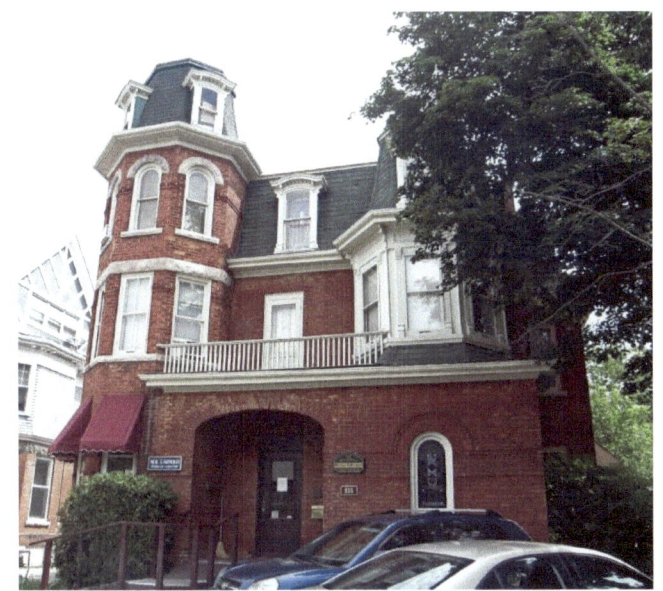

Owen Sound Book 2 - #935 2nd Avenue West – built in 1912, Second Empire style, 3-storey turret, mansard roof

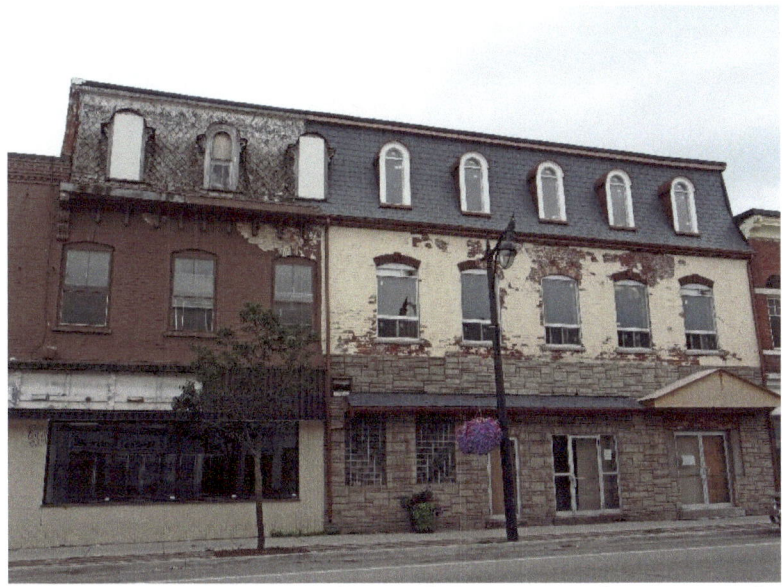

Palmerston - Main Street – Second Empire style, mansard roof with dormers

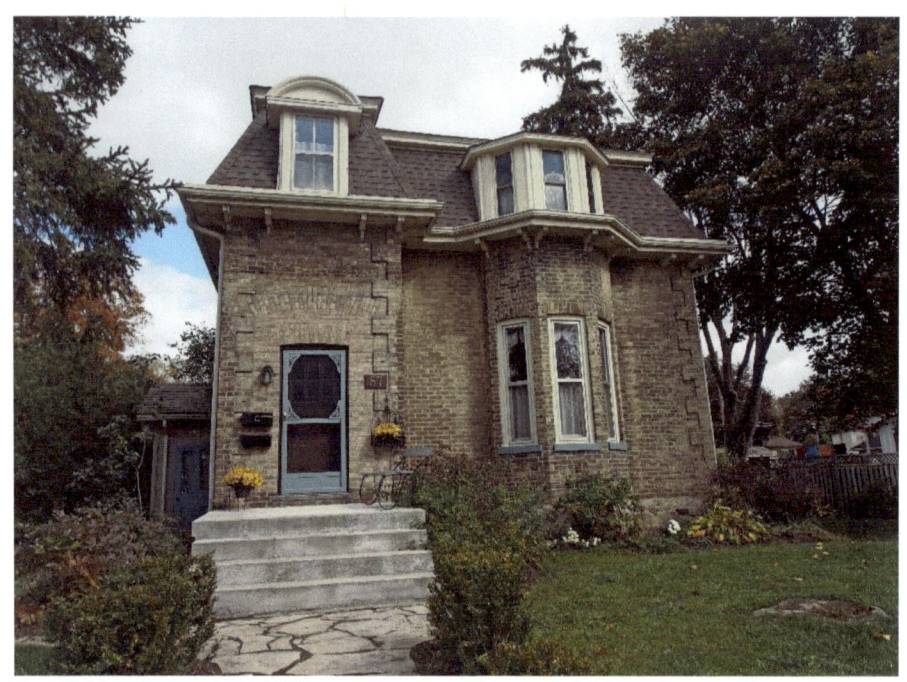

Paris Book 3 - 87 Willow Street – Second Empire style – mansard roof, tall windows, dormers

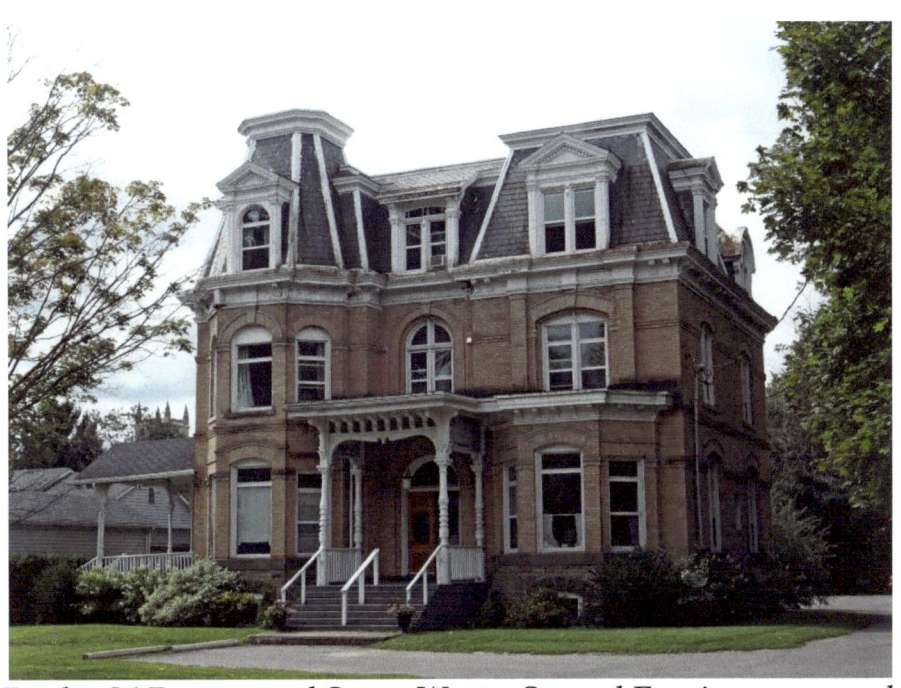

Perth - 26 Drummond Street West – Second Empire – mansard roof, dormers with window hoods, tower, voussoirs and keystones, turned veranda roof supports with decorative capitals

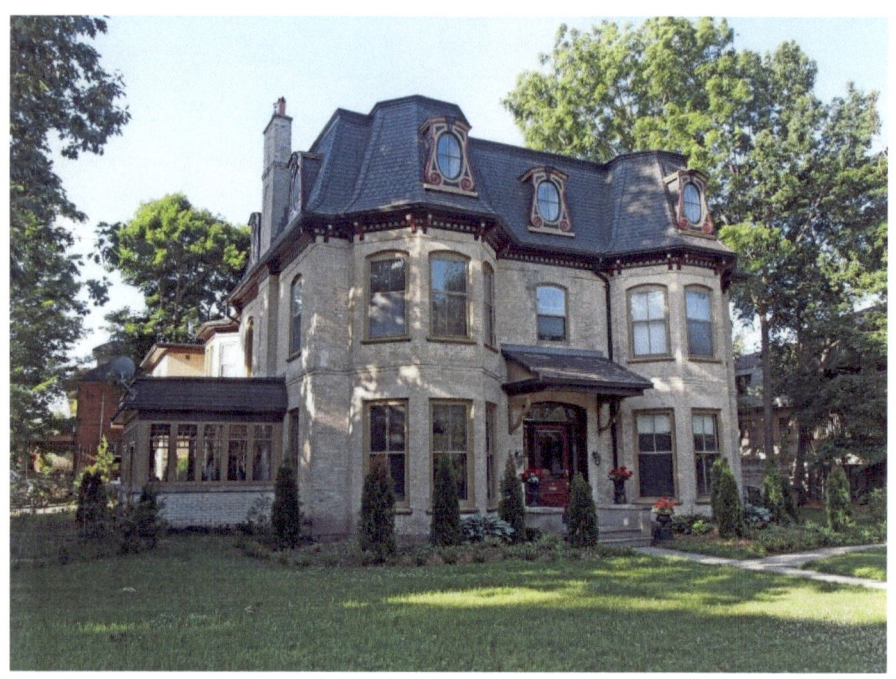
Peterborough Book 1 - 359 Downie Street – Second Empire style, mansard roof, window hoods, 2 storey bay windows

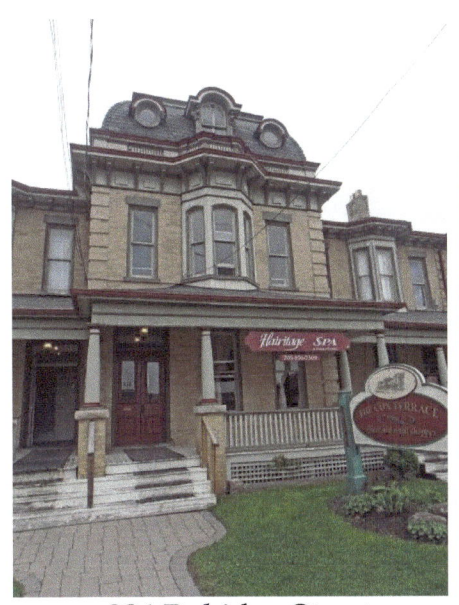 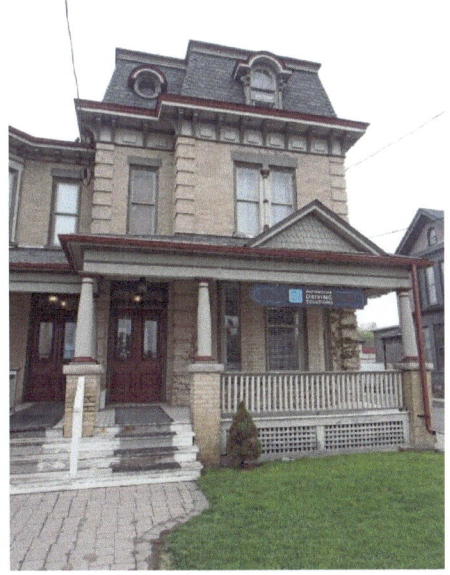

334 Rubidge Street   332 Rubidge Street

Peterborough Book 2 - An elegant example of a residential terrace in the Second Empire style, Cox Terrace, 332-344 Rubidge Street, was constructed in 1884 during a time of prosperity and rapid urban growth in Peterborough. In this row of houses, inspired by British models, seven dwellings are skillfully unified behind one façade with three projecting pavilions. Mansard roofs, dormers, and oriel windows give life to the distinctive design. The terrace was built for Sir George Cox, one of the wealthiest and most influential Canadian businessmen of the period.

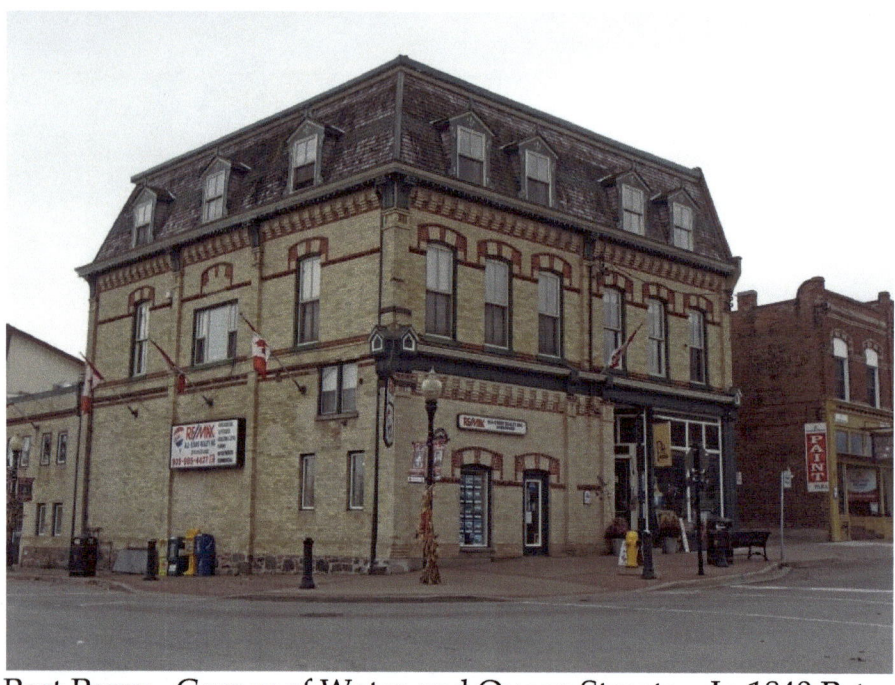

Port Perry - Corner of Water and Queen Streets – In 1840 Peter Perry purchased forty acres in downtown Port Perry and in 1844 he built a frame building which house a store, trading post, and a home for his agent, Chester Draper. Immediately after Perry's death is 1851, the property was bought by Mason and Phillips who turned it into a hotel. Henry Charles purchased it in 1867. The present yellow building was built after the fire of 1884. The hotel had thirty rooms including a dining room and at the street level were two stores including a sample room where salesmen could display their wares. They named it the St. Charles Hotel after Henry Charles.

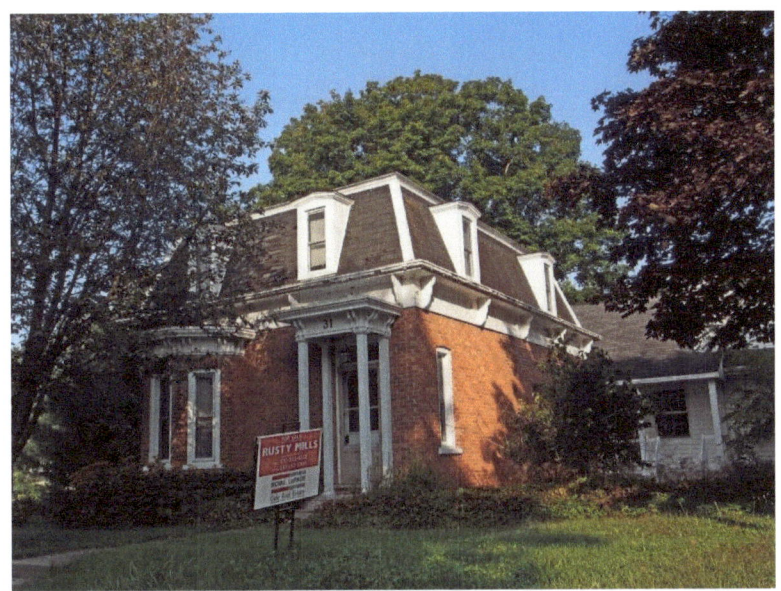

Portland, Newboro Book – Newboro - #31 - Second Empire – mansard roof with dormers, cornice brackets, bay window

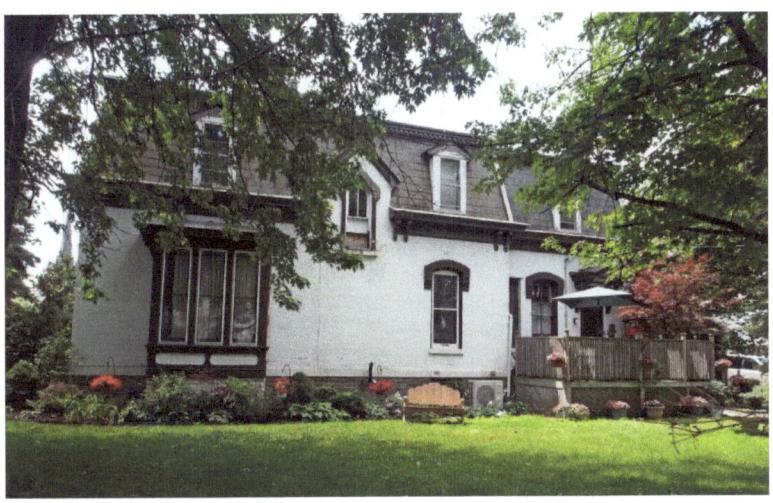

Sarnia Book 4 – 289 Vidal Street North – 1870 – Second Empire style, mansard roof with dormers, cornice brackets, dentil moulding, rectangular bay window, voussoirs

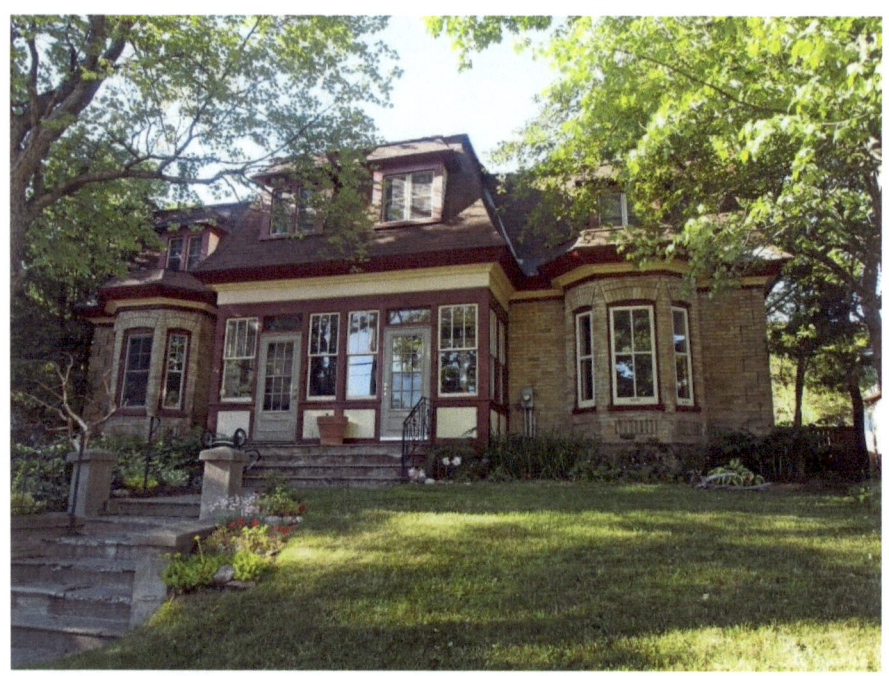

Sault Ste. Marie - Built in 1889, 34-36 Herrick Street is a yellow brick residence located on a quiet dead-end street in the east end of the older residential core of Sault Ste. Marie. This house is an early example of Second Empire style architecture. The south elevation of the main house faces the street and was built in a symmetrical fashion. It is heightened by a projecting central frontispiece that continues up into a mansard roof which was originally sheathed with cedar shingles. Around the turn of the century, a demising wall was constructed through the middle of the house and the front porch was rebuilt to accommodate separate front entrances for two semi-detached units.

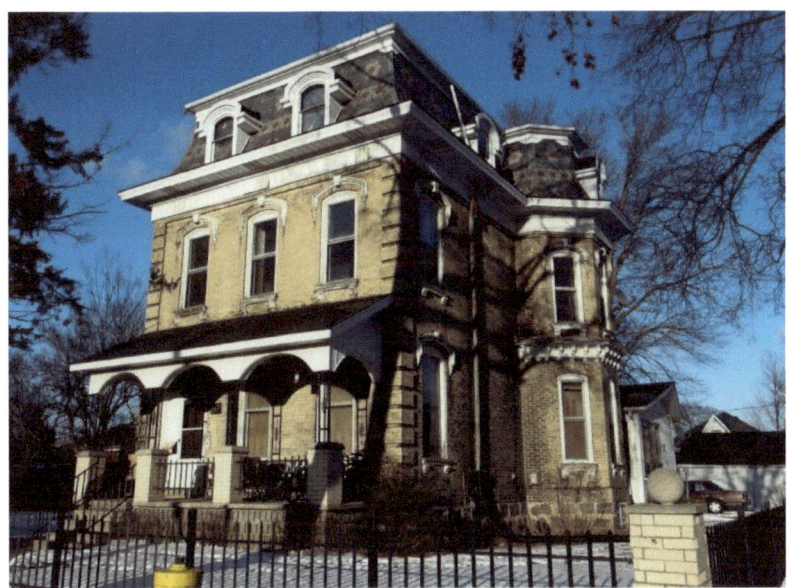

Simcoe - 217 Colborne Street – Second Empire style – mansard roof, dichromatic tilework

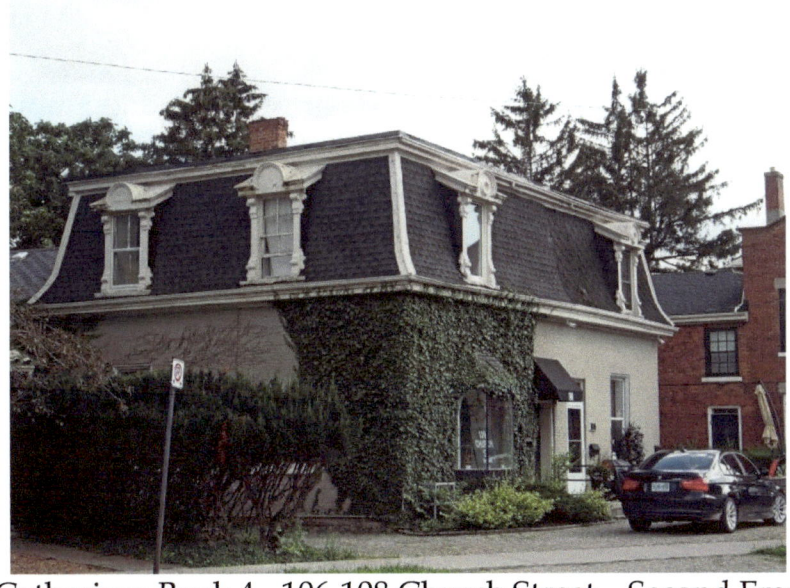

St. Catharines Book 4 - 106-108 Church Street – Second Empire style, mansard roof, dormers with window hoods

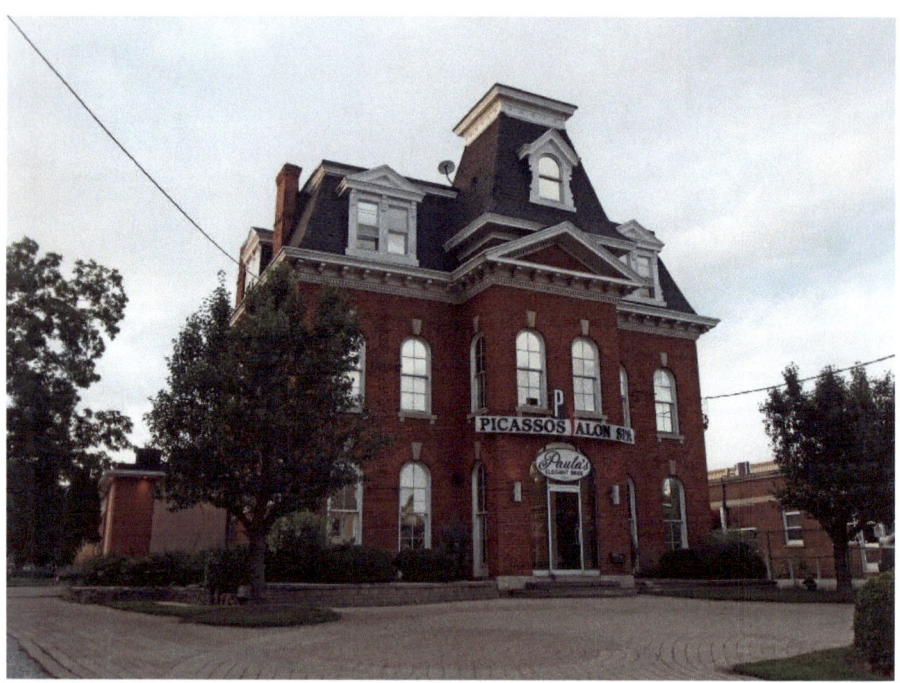

St. Catharines Book 5 - 15 Welland Avenue – Second Empire – mansard roof with dormers with window hoods, three-storey tower, pediment, cornice brackets, voussoirs and keystones

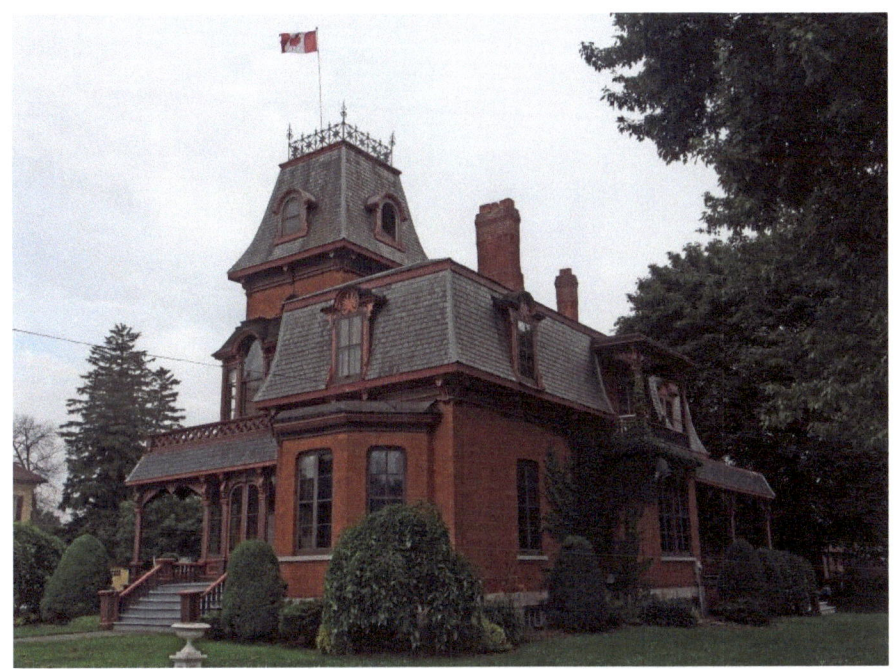

St. Marys Book 1 - 236 Jones Street East - Ercildoune was originally built as a wedding gift to George Carter's daughter Charlotte when she married Henry Lincoln Rice in 1880. The home is built in the Second Empire style, a very rare style of home in St. Marys.

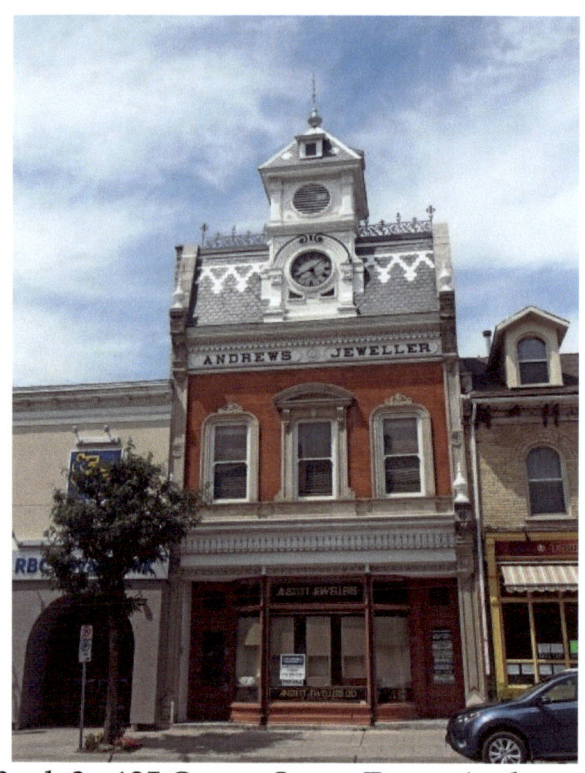

St. Marys Book 2 - 135 Queen Street East – Andrews Block built in 1884 – large two storeys with clock tower – Second Empire style – richly ornamented façade – white brick trimmed with red

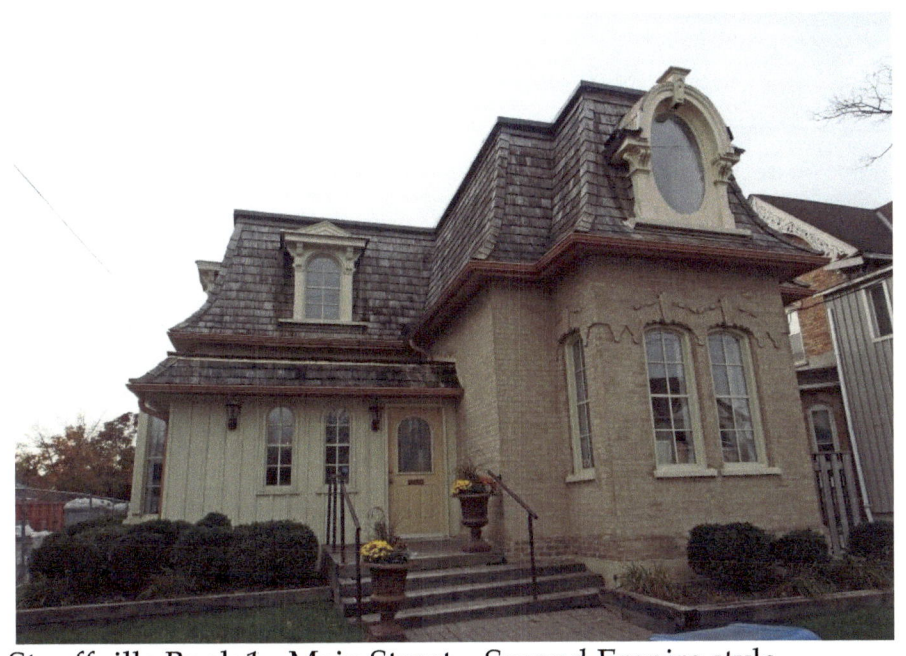

Stouffville Book 1 - Main Street – Second Empire style - mansard roof, dormers with window hoods

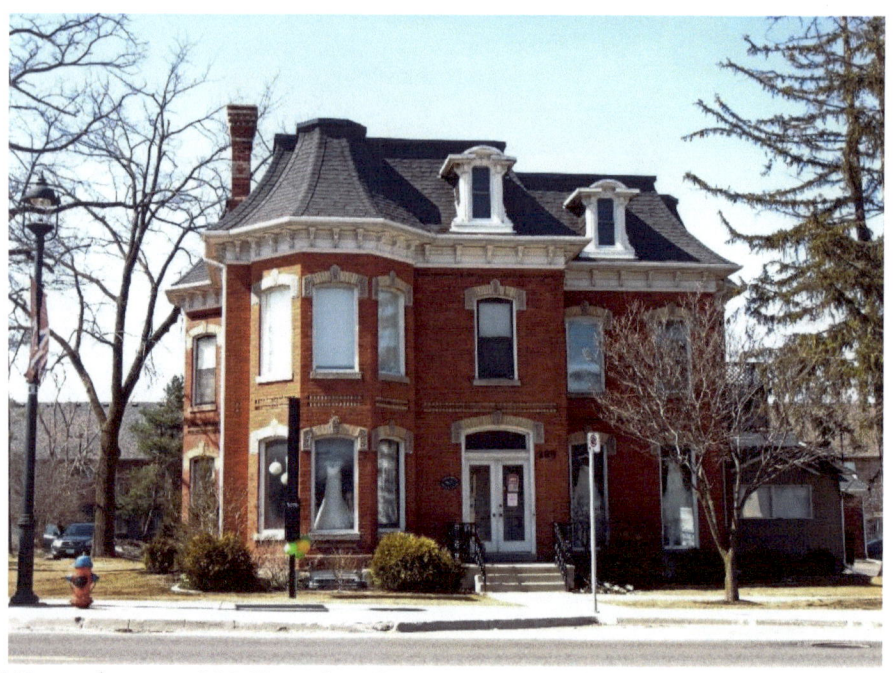

Waterdown - 299 Dundas Street – Second Empire style, mansard roof, dormers in roof, cornice brackets, two-storey tower-like bays

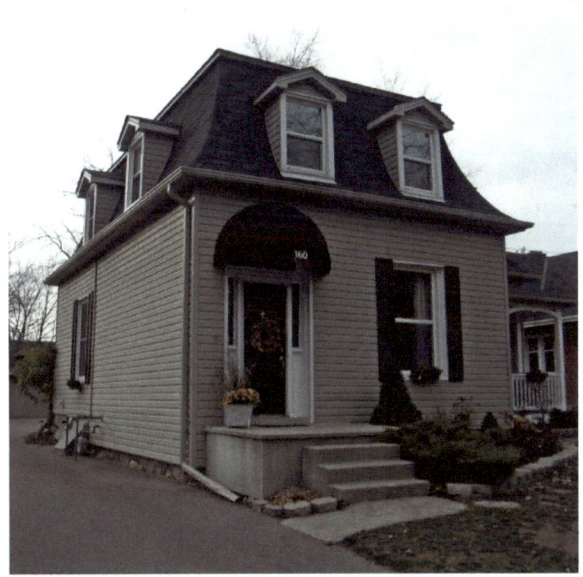

Waterford - 160 Main Street – Second Empire style, mansard roof, dormers

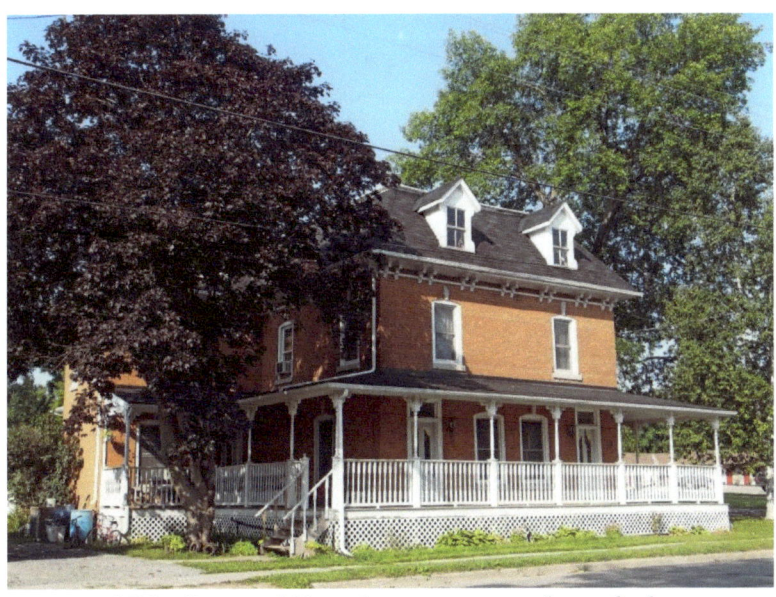

Westport - #56 - Second Empire – mansard roof, dormers, veranda pillars with decorative capitals, open railing, cornice brackets, voussoirs and keystones, transom windows

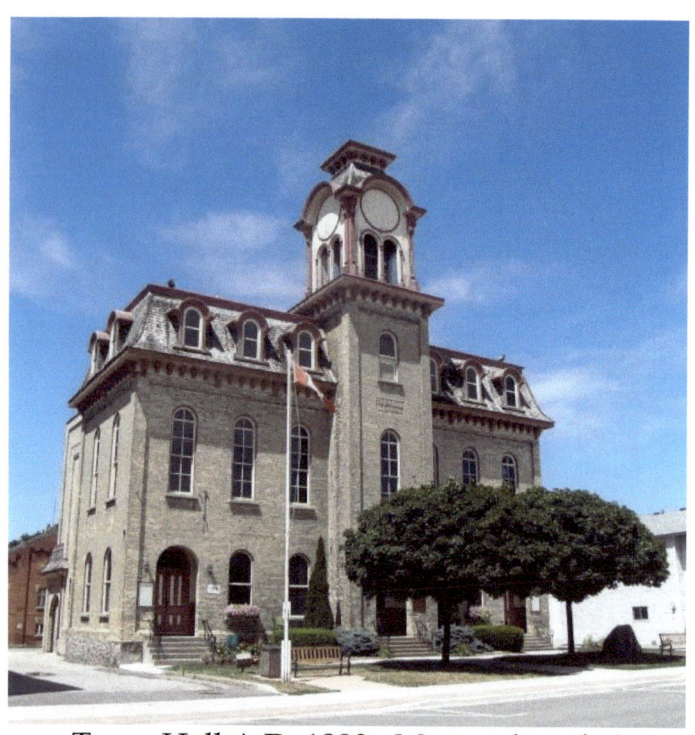

Wingham - Town Hall A.D. 1890 - Mansard roof, dormers, cornice brackets

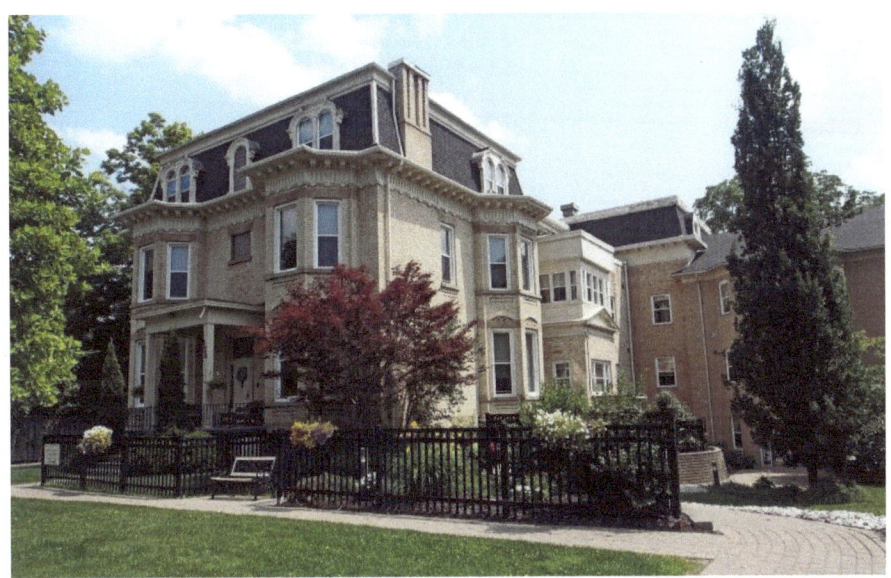

Woodstock Book 1 - 126 Graham Street – c. 1860 - Second Empire - symmetrical three-story white brick, mansard roof, dentils, decorative cornice with large brackets, two-story bay windows flank entrance, decorated cut stone lintels, rough faced stone lintels second floor, dormers have decorative wooden frames, large front door is flanked by transom and side lights, an open portico protects the entrance – now Park Place Retirement Centre

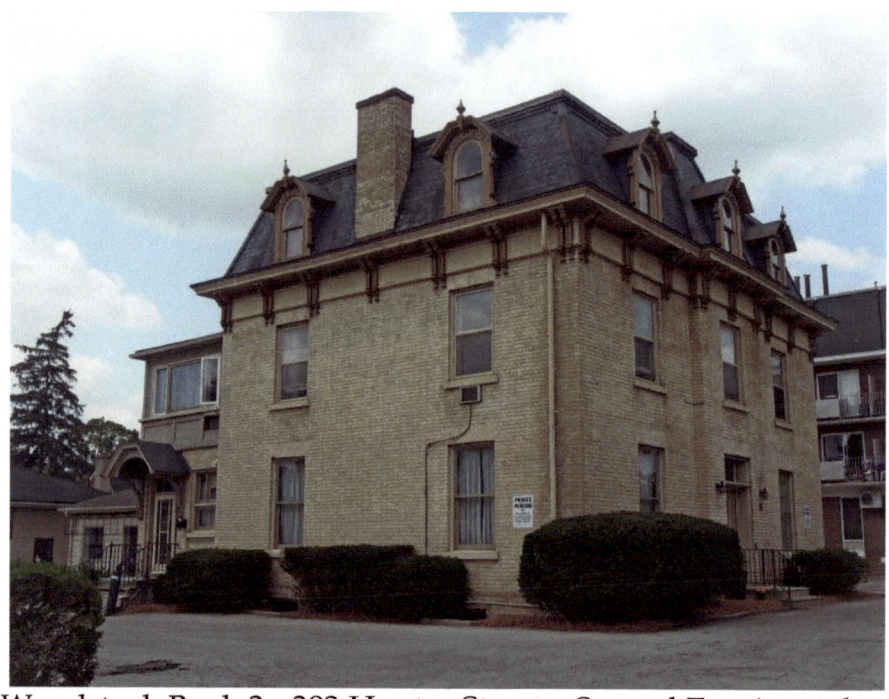

Woodstock Book 3 - 393 Hunter Street – Second Empire style – mansard roof with dormers with finials on window hoods, cornice brackets

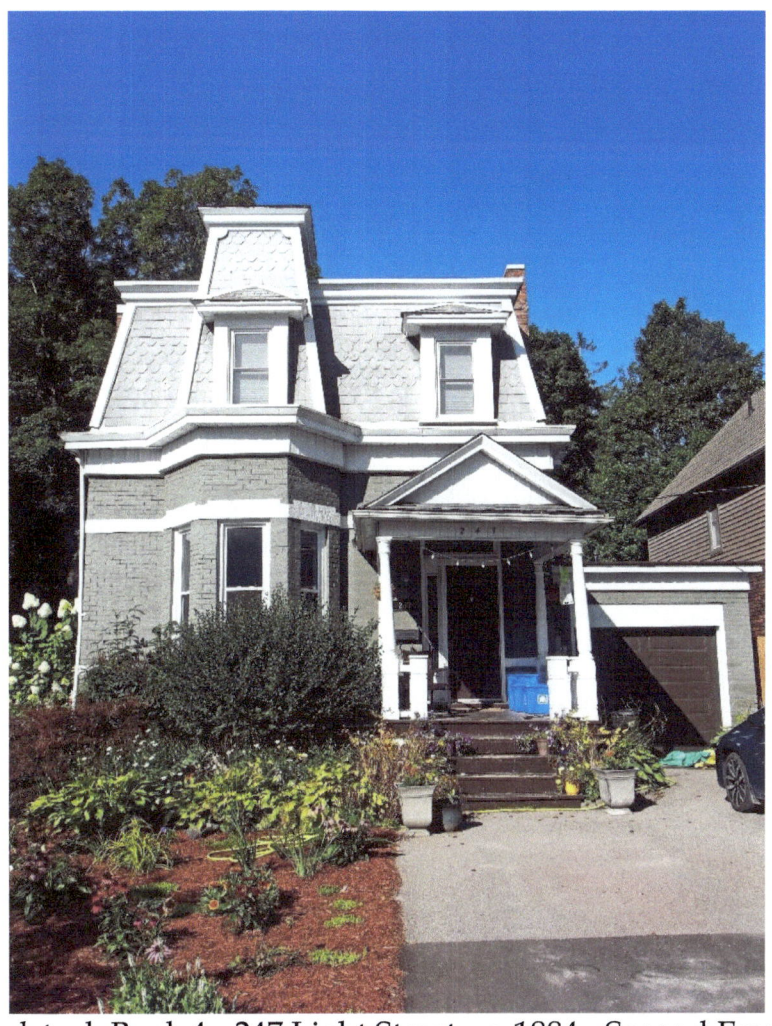

Woodstock Book 4 - 247 Light Street - c. 1884 - Second Empire, two story, red brick (painted), decorated painted wood shingles on Mansard roof, brick string course and recessed bricking beneath 1st story bay window, double front door with transom is protected by new porch, cut field stone foundation

Other Books by Barbara Raue

Coins of Gold
Arrows, Indians and Love
The Life and Times of Barbara
The Cromwell Family Book
Laura Secord Discovered
Daddy Where Are You?

Montana Series
Book 1: Montana Dream
Book 2: Life on the Montana Frontier
Book 3: Montana to Boston and Back
Book 4: Montana Sons Go to War
Book 5: Montana Sons Return from War

Book 1: Rite of Passage
Book 2: Rite of Marriage

© 2019 by Barbara Raue - All the photos in this book have been taken with my cameras. I own the rights to them.

Barbara is The Authority on Saving Our History One Photo at a Time. She is pursuing her interest in photography and architecture by preserving a record through photos of old buildings from the 1800s and 1900s with their unique architecture. Enjoy the beautiful architecture in the comfort of your living room. Dream about what it was like in those by-gone days. Dream about what it was like to live in a mansion like one of those in this book.

Barbara Raue, a wife, mother and grandmother, is an avid reader and writer. She has researched and compiled several family histories. In 2010, Barbara published her book "Coins of Gold," which celebrates the courageous life of her mother, May Todd. Barbara's second book is a historical fiction "Arrows, Indians and Love" which takes place in Boonesborough, Kentucky during the time of Daniel Boone. In 2013, Barbara published *The Cromwell Family Book* in which she traces her ancestry generations back into Great Britain. Her second novel is called *Laura Secord Discovered,* in which the story of Laura's service during the War of 1812 is shared. Barbara's memoir is titled *Daddy Where Are You?* It tells of her life growing up without a father. Five novels in the Montana Series have been published, *Montana Dream, Life on the Montana Frontier, Montana to Boston and Back, Montana Sons Go to War*, and *Montana Sons Return from War*. *Rite of Passage* and *Rite of Marriage* is a two-book series.

This is a link to Barbara's website to view all of her books
http://barbararaue.ca

www.ingramcontent.com/pod-product-compliance
Lightning Source LLC
Chambersburg PA
CBHW040238220526
45473CB00001B/283